Innovations and Organizations

INNOVATIONS
AND ORGANIZATIONS

GERALD ZALTMAN

ROBERT DUNCAN

JONNY HOLBEK

A Wiley-Interscience Publication

JOHN WILEY & SONS
New York · London · Sydney · Toronto

TO Hugh and Nora Moodie
Stephanie and Christopher
The Baums for their friendship

Printed in the United States of America
10 9 8 7 6 5 4 3 2 1

Copyright © 1973, by John Wiley & Sons, Inc.

All rights reserved. Published simultaneously in Canada.

Library of Congress Cataloging in Publication Data:

Zaltman, Gerald.
    Innovations and organizations.

    "A Wiley-Interscience publication."
    Bibliography: p.
    1. Organizational change.   2. Diffusion of innova-
tions.   I. Duncan, Robert, 1942–   joint author.
II. Holbek, Jonny, joint author.   III. Title.

HM131.Z32   301.24'8   73-5873

ISBN 0-471-98129-X

PREFACE

The major impetus for preparing this book stemmed from the frustration we experienced with our students in trying to find a relatively brief but balanced treatment of the adoption of innovations in organizations. We particularly sensed the lack of material that integrated findings on innovation in different types of organizations. Consequently we pooled efforts to develop a document that could serve as a primer on innovations in organizations for courses related to social change, management, organizational behavior, and marketing at both the advanced undergraduate and graduate levels. The outcome is the present book, which has three basic objectives:

1. To provide the student with a brief overview of the research on innovations, specifically on the types of innovations and the variables and conditions affecting the process of innovation adoption by organizations.

2. To focus on the innovation-adoption process as it takes place within multimember units of adoption. Most of the literature on innovation has centered on single-member adopter units. In this book we discuss the innovation and diffusion process in multimember units. Thus this book stresses the characteristics of organizations in terms of structures and processes that facilitate and inhibit innovation.

3. To look at the environment within which the innovation-adoption process takes place and the kinds of environments that are conducive to the introduction and diffusion of innovations.

We make no pretense to have covered all the relevant literature in depth. Our focus, rather, has been to present a general overview, providing guidelines to sources, where they exist, that treat particular topics in some depth. With this goal in mind there is an extensive bibliography.

We would like to acknowledge the helpful comments of Richard Clewett, Robert Cooke, and Edward Watson, who read the manuscript at various stages of development. We would also like to thank Michael Radnor for his support and encouragement during the preparation of the manuscript. However, we alone are responsible for any omissions, deletions, or errors in what appears here.

We would also like to acknowledge the generous support of the Graduate School of Management, Northwestern University, and the Health Services Research Center, which is a joint program of Northwestern University and the Hospital Research and Educational Trust of the American Hospital Association. The HSRC provided valuable research support to one of the authors during the preparation of this manuscript.

GERALD ZALTMAN

Graduate School of Management
Northwestern University
Evanston, Illinois

ROBERT DUNCAN

Graduate School of Management
Northwestern University
Evanston, Illinois

JONNY HOLBEK

University of Trondheim
Trondheim, Norway

February 1973

CONTENTS

1 The Nature of Innovations

CONTENTS

INTRODUCTION

It is useful, initially, to present an overview of the total change process as it relates to organizations and to draw a number of distinctions between terms and ideas that are used throughout this book. To begin, there is the social milieu, which consists of two levels, within which the organization exists. The first level of this social milieu or megasystem is the general industry, for example, a field of education, the iron and steel industry, public health, of which the individual organization is a part. That the industry is a relevant and viable social system in itself has been well documented (most recently by Czepiel, 1972). Components of this system include competing firms, customers, trade associations, unions, relevant governmental regulating agencies, and suppliers. These components provide the immediate external environment of the organization. The second-level environment is society in general, including those sectors of the economy that indirectly influence the well-being of the particular industry, for example, general governmental activity, the education sector which provides the needed skills, and the level and nature of activity in science and technology in general which influence production methods, or new product opportunities.

This second-level milieu encompasses the first, which in turn encompasses the organization. Changes in the structure and functioning of either level, but especially in level one, constitute social change, which may create performance gaps (the concept of performance gaps is discussed in some detail in Chapter 2). Social change "is the process by which alteration occurs in the structure and function of a social system" (Rogers, 1969). Performance gaps are discrepancies between what the organization could do by virtue of a goal-related opportunity in its environment and what it actually does in terms of exploiting that opportunity. The performance gap may be characterized by new marketing opportunities brought about by changes among consumers, or by loss of market because of new competition. The performance gap may also occur when new technical specifications are required by governmental regulatory agencies. In these and many other cases a change has occurred in the structure and/or functioning of the megasystem, creating or widening a gap between the organization's current performance and its normative performance in light of the changes in the external environment. A performance gap may be increased by changes within the organization, such as when a key expert on some part of the environment permanently leaves the organization.

The performance gap may persist for some time before it is recognized; in fact, it may never be recognized. Given the assumption that the organization is aware of the gap, a need can be said to exist. This involves another assumption: the performance gap is perceived as having significant adverse consequences for the organization if the gap is not narrowed or bridged. The awareness and need, in effect, unfreeze elements within the organization most closely related to the external environmental change. When this occurs, conditions are present for altering the structure and function of the organization or some subsystem of it. It is also possible, of course, that a change can be imposed on an organization even in the absence of needs for change. Union demands and government or court decisions concerning mergers, are examples. For our purposes, however, we do not focus on such changes.

This need changes the social-psychological state of the organization by unfreezing some elements of the organization. One manifestation of this action is a search for means to close the performance gap. The search can be both internal and external. Internally it may involve determining whether the organization already has the solution to the performance gap, or at least has the means or resources to develop a solution independent of agencies or resource persons outside the organization. Externally, the organization may also adopt or adapt a solution already in existence, or it may commission appropriate research-and-development work to obtain the necessary object.

At the next stage, alternative solutions, if indeed there are alternatives, are identified. Given these alternative ideas, practices, or products, a decision-making process is undertaken by the relevant group or person within the organization, perhaps with the assistance of outside advice. Decision making can be defined as "a conscious and human process, involving both individual and social phenomena, based upon factual and value premises, which concludes with a choice of one behavioral activity from among one or more alternatives with the intention of moving toward some desired state of affairs" (Shull et al., 1970, p. 31). In studying decision making in health organizations, Roos and Berlin (1972) state that when a decision style that seeks compromises is characteristic, the search for alternatives will be short and the number of decision alternatives small. When a maximizing decision style is dominant, the search will be long and the number of alternatives large. One can infer from their proposition that under a decision style that seeks compromises the first acceptable innovation will be adopted, in contrast to the maximizing style, which stresses adoption of the most-favorable innovation.

All these factors are displayed in Figure 1-1. Additional figures and discussion elaborating upon the cells in Figure 1-1 are presented throughout this book at appropriate points. Figure 1-1 in the general form presented is descriptive of change processes in most organizations. This includes profit and nonprofit organizations as well as private and public organizations.

The innovation can precede and cause social change, or it may be developed in response to needs created by social change. There is a continuous and dynamic interaction between new ideas, practices, and products on the one hand and

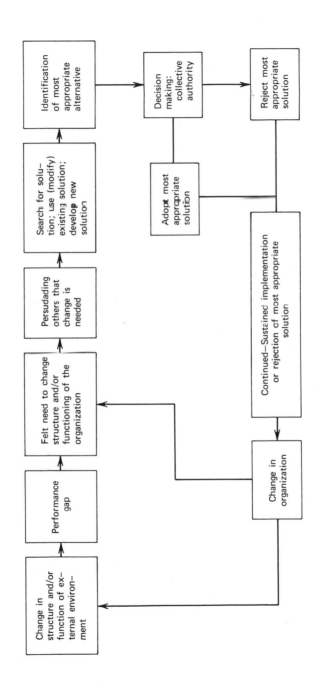

Figure 1-1. Paradigm of organizational change and innovation.

social structure and function on the other hand. Innovations can create social change, and the subsequent social change can bring about additional innovations that can react back upon altered structures and/or functions which brought them into existence or which influence other aspects of the organization. New ideas can originate from within or from without the social system. A paradigm describing this has been developed by Everett Rogers (1969, p. 6); although the paradigm (shown here in Table 1-1) was originally for large communities, it applies equally well to formal organizations of a different nature.

Table 1-1.   Paradigm of Types of Social Change

Recognition of Need for Change	Origin of the New Idea	
	Internal to Social System	External to Social System
Internal: recognition is by members of the social system	I. Immanent change	II. Selective contact change
External: recognition may be by change agents outside the social system	III. Motivated immanent change	IV. Directed contact change

(From Rogers, 1969)

The idea component of social change is the concern of this chapter. The importance of new ideas cannot be understated. Ideas and their manifestations as practices or products are at the core of social change. An idea stimulates a decision-making process by some social unit (e.g., an individual, hospital, or business firm) which in turn eventually produces a change in the structure and/or function of that unit and perhaps even causes changes in the environment of the decision-making unit. The resulting change brings other new ideas into being, although there may not always be a need for them. In many instances, however, the need does exist and is the driving force bringing new ideas, or what will shortly be called innovative solutions, into being. In the subsequent discussion we are concerned exclusively with new ideas, that is, innovations. Let us now turn our attention to that subject.

THE INNOVATION

The term *innovation* is usually employed in three different contexts (see Tilton, 1971, pp. 4 6). In one context it is synonymous with invention; that is, it refers to a creative process whereby two or more existing concepts or entities are combined in some novel way to produce a configuration not previously known by the person involved. A person or organization performing this type of activity is usually said to be innovative. Most of the literature on creativity treats the term innovation in this fashion (e.g., Steiner, 1965; National Academy of Sciences, 1969).

Myers and Marquis (1969) use innovation in this fashion, with an emphasis upon technological development.

"A technical innovation is a complex activity which proceeds from the conceptualization of a new idea to a solution of the problem and then to the actual utilization of a new item of economic or social value. (Alternatively) innovation is not a single action but a total process of interrelated subprocesses. It is not just the conception of a new idea, nor the invention of a new device, nor the development of a new market. The process is all of these things acting in an integrated fashion . . ." (p. 1).

This view of innovation as a process starting with the recognition of a potential demand for, and technical feasibility of, an item and ending with its widespread utilization is perhaps the broadest use of the term innovation in the existing literature. It blends the idea of invention with that of adoption.

Innovation is also used to describe only the process whereby an existing innovation becomes a part of an adopter's cognitive state and behavioral repertoire. This is a process of adoption and internationalization. For example, Knight (1967, p. 478) offers the following definition: "An innovation is the adoption of a change which is new to an organization and to the relevant environment." Mohr (1969) follows a similar approach in defining the term innovation as "the successful introduction into an applied situation of means or ends that are new to that situation" (p. 112). Mohr's noting of means or ends and situations anticipates an extended discussion of innovative situations and solutions to follow shortly. Knight (1967) considers the process of innovation "as a special case of the process of change in an organization. The two differ only in the novelty of the outcome" (p. 479). This view of innovation is the subject of Chapter 2.

In the first usage of innovation the individual or organization can be innovative without adopting; whereas in the present case he can be innovative without being inventive. It is acknowledged, however, that one could argue that the adoption or internalization of an innovation might be viewed as an inventive activity because two previously unconnected constructs, the individual or organization and the innovation, are combined in some novel way.

The third use of the term is to refer to that idea, practice, or material artifact that has been invented or that is regarded as novel independent of its adoption or nonadoption. The emphasis here is on description of why something is novel, whereas invention and adoption involve processes. This chapter focuses on this third notion, that is, on the description of relevant attributes and dimensions of innovations.

Barnett (1953) views an innovation broadly by emphasizing objectively measurable qualitative differences. According to Barnett, an innovation is "any thought, behavior or thing that is new because it is qualitatively different from existing forms" (p. 7). He goes on to emphasize the distinction between thought, behavior, and thing. "Strictly speaking, every innovation is an idea, or a constellation of ideas; but some innovations by their nature must remain mental organizations only, whereas others may be given overt and tangible expression" (p. 7).

Similarly, Hagen (1962, p. 87) has commented that there is no such thing as innovation in the abstract. It is always in some specific field, involving specific materials or concepts, or relationships to other persons. He defines an innovation as an organization of reality into relationships embodying new mental or esthetic concepts, with the new relationships being an improvement over the old.

The Federal Trade Commission has emphasized Barnett's definition in an advisory opinion stating that consumer and industrial products can be called "new" only when they are either entirely new or have been changed in a functionally significant and substantial respect (Federal Trade Commission, 1967). Others have defined as innovations only those ideas, products, or services that have not yet secured more than 10% acceptance within the relevant social system (Bell, 1963). Robertson (1971) has suggested that the critical factor in defining an item as an innovation should be its effect upon established patterns of consumption or behavior. He suggests three possible patterns of effect. An innovation that has little disruptive impact on behavior patterns is called a continuous innovation: a PERT flow chart is an example. In this case the item constitutes only slight alteration of a current practice. Next are those innovations, dynamically continuous innovations, that have a moderate impact on behavior patterns, for example, the continuous casting process adopted by firms in the steel industry. Finally, there are discontinuous innovations that involve the establishment of new behavior patterns, such as team teaching, T-groups, and the provision of human sexuality programs by family planning personnel.

In this volume we consider as an innovation *any idea, practice, or material artifact perceived to be new by the relevant unit of adoption.* The adopting unit can vary from a single individual to a business firm, a city (Crain, 1966), or a state legislature (Walker, 1969). This position is very similar to the stance taken by Rogers and Shoemaker (1971, p. 19):

> "An innovation is an idea, practice, or object perceived as new by the individual. It matters little, as far as human behavior is concerned, whether or not an idea is 'objectively' new as measured by the lapse of time since its first use or discovery . . . If the idea seems new and different to the individual, it is an innovation."

Our definition differs from Rogers primarily in that the unit of adoption may be larger than an individual, which also means that not all members of an organization may think of the item as an innovation. One implication of this is the possibility of conflict between those in the organization who view the object or practice in question as an innovation and tend to resist change and those who perceive of it as not significantly new and advocate adoption of the product or practice (see Evans, 1970; Goodenough, 1963; Dymsza, 1972). This, of course, assumes a context of conservative management.

The value of this definition, emphasizing what the adoption unit perceives, is that it applies equally well to both static and dynamic populations. For example, Bennett (1969) has distinguished between *innovativeness* (how soon an existing member of a group adopts the item or innovation after its initial appearance) and *precocity* (the speed of acceptance of an item by an individual after his entry into a group in which an innovation already exists and may have been widely accepted). Other definitions do not apply very well in dynamic organizations were precocity is an important factor.

Treatments of innovations vis-a-vis organizations tend to

follow the individual-oriented approaches which emphasize newness. For example, Walker (1969) in his study of the diffusion of ideas for new services or programs in the United States, defines an innovation as ". . . a program or policy which is new to the states adopting it, no matter how old the program may be or how many other states may have adopted it" (p. 881). Similarly, Gross, Giacquinta, and Bernstein (1971) define an organizational innovation as "any proposed idea, or set of ideas, about how the organizational behavior of members should be changed in order to resolve problems of the organization or to improve its performance" (p. 16). For Gross et al., the length of time the idea has been in existence and the number of other organizations that have adopted it do not directly affect its newness to the organization considering its adoption. Hage and Aiken (1970, pp. 13–14) follow an essentially similar approach. For them an innovation, that is, a program change, is defined as "the addition of new services or products . . . This does not imply that each new program adopted by an organization is necessarily new to the society. A particular new program may be new only to the organization being studied."

Not all authors agree with this approach. For example, Becker and Whisler (1967, p. 463) although talking about innovation as a process, suggest "defining innovation as the first or early use of an idea by one of a set of organizations with similar goals." Here we see an emphasis upon how *new* an idea is *to the environment* rather than the individual organization. According to Becker and Whisler, organizational innovation occurs when the organization is among the first to adopt and incurs significant costs of search and risk. A firm adopting later, that is, after a significant number of other persons adopt and some time has elapsed, undergoes organizational change but not innovation, whereas the early adopting organizations undergo both innovation and change. Implicit in Becker and Whisler's position is the assumption that a given change involves an innovation process only when it occurs early in the diffusion process of the item.

Wilson (1966, p. 196), speaking in an organizational context, defines an innovation in the following way: "An innovation (or, more precisely, a major innovation, since we are not concerned with trivial changes) is a 'fundamental' change in a 'significant' number of tasks." (Note here that Wilson emphasizes the *impact* of an idea as a basis for defining it as an innovation.) Importantly, Wilson adds:

> What is "fundamental" and "significant" cannot be given a precise definition, for in our scheme the meaning of these terms can only be determined by the organizations themselves. Each organization, we assume, can rank proposed (or actual) changes in terms of how "radical" they will be (or are) . . . The greater the cost in scarce inducements, the more radical the innovation, regardless of the prospective benefits (pp. 196–197).

Here again we notice an emphasis on the perceptions of the potential unit of adoption. However, recall Knight's phrase "new to the organization and to the *relevant environment*" (italics added). This introduces the notion that the idea must also be new to the *reference group* of an organization.

The issues of how organizations—informal and formal —perceive things and the issue of measuring such perceptions is a very neglected area of research. However, these issues must still be faced. As with individuals, many factors can affect how an organization views environmental stimuli that may be classified as innovations. We offer, very tentatively, the following as an example: the age of the organization influences its history of experiences with potential innovations and hence influences how familiar the practice or product is. This is quite related to another factor, namely the length of time key employees have been in the industry; that is, the longer they have been in the industry, the better able they may be to determine actual, objective dissimilarity between the item in question and some previously existing item. This suggests that all those factors influencing individual perceptions of innovation directly or indirectly influence the organization's perception. Although the number of other organizations adopting an idea is not, for purposes in this book, a direct basis for classifying that idea as an innovation, it may be indirectly influential to the extent that a firm's perception of what is new is a function of how many other firms or organizations have adopted it. An organization's identification with another firm that has adopted the idea may constitute symbolic adoption for the organization so that when actual adoption occurs, the idea is, in fact, very familiar or at least not new. This also suggests that where imitative behavior occurs among organizations, newness is perceived by the imitating organizations at the time the early adopting organization first adopts. Of course, all these ideas need testing. Many more factors could be listed. The important point for our purposes is that organizations, like individuals, have perceptions and that the nature of their perceptual processes is particularly important—and poorly understood at present —for studying the adoption or rejection of innovations by organizations (Tilton, 1971).

One caveat should be added here concerning the use of perception of the unit of adoption as a criterion for defining innovativeness: perception varies according to the physiological state of the individual and according to the different contextual situations the adopting unit may be in. It may also vary over time according to the adoption process stage. For example, when an executive or buying committee has only limited knowledge of an item, it may not be seen as an innovation. As further information is accumulated and attitudes toward the object formed or changed, the executive may develop a new perception in which the object is cast as an innovation. The reverse can also take place. An item initially thought of as new may over the course of the decision-making process lose its character of being significantly unique.

This can occur for at least two reasons. On closer inspection the buying committee may conclude that the item is not so new after all. Additionally, as the decision process becomes protracted and the innovation gains acceptance and becomes a part of the social milieu, the executive or buying committee through sheer familiarity with the item may cease to perceive of it as new.

To sum up the discussion thus far, the distinguishing characteristic of an innovation is that instead of being an external object, it is the perception of a social unit that decides its newness. Thus a practice can be an innovation for one organization but not for another. The process by which an innovation is spread through communication channels to members of a social system, for example, firms in an industry, over time is called diffusion. When an innovation is diffused and adopted (either symbolically or behaviorally) by a sufficient number of the relevant units in a social system to register an impact (becoming an integrated part of the normative patterns in the system) it is said that a social change has occurred in the system under discussion.

Knight (1967) and Knight and Wind (1968) note that innovations appear in or are relevant to four aspects of organization. First, they may pertain to the product or services performed by the organization. The decision of a clinic to offer financial incentives to encourage family planning (Rogers, 1973) or a health agency to perform vasectomies (Zaltman, 1972), the decision of a firm to offer trading stamps (Allvine, 1968) or to enter a new market are examples. Second, innovations may be production-process oriented. Examples are the use of the Stirling cycle (Koëhler, 1969), adoption of the continuous casting process in the steel industry (Czepiel, 1972), the use of a code conversion device by railroads (Myers and Marquis, 1969), and automated assembly lines. Another example might include changes in an accounting process. These all involve changes in the organization's task systems or in its physical production operations. Third are the organizational-structure innovations such as decentralizing decision making, instituting incentive systems, managerial grid seminars (Blake and Mouton, 1969), management training units (Hutchins, 1972), and the introduction of change teams in education (Coughlan and Zaltman, 1972). Fourth are people innovations such as programs on creative decision making (Kepner and Tregoe, 1960), T-groups (Golembiewski and Blumberg 1970), and the use of social research to improve social practice (Lippitt, 1965). Organizational-structural and people innovations are commented on briefly again further in this chapter. It is obvious that the four aspects or contexts just mentioned are highly interrelated and that the successful implementation of an innovation along one aspect depends on how well changes are made along other aspects. For example, one business firm in the clothing industry decided to expand its operations to household furnishings (a product innovation). This was accomplished by a merger (an organizational-structure change) with a smaller firm already in the household furnishings industry. T-group sessions (people-related innovation) were used at the time of the merger to reduce anticipated personnel conflicts resulting from the consolidation of the management staffs of the two companies. Another example of interrelatedness is provided by a family planning clinic that decided to offer a specialized new service, abortion counseling. This new service was perceived by some of the staff as a threat to their relative positions of power (a change in structural relations). Eventually two of those most opposed to the new service were replaced by more sympathetic individuals. This action qualifies as a people innovation as described by Knight. The addition of abortion counselors also represented a people innovation.

A very important area of organizational innovation not covered by Knight's classification concerns policy innovation, which is a sufficient but not necessary condition preceding any other type of change. Policy innovations involve major changes in the organization's strategies for achieving its major objectives. In the health field the decision of family planning groups to use adopter and diffuser incentives is widely considered as a major policy innovation (see Rogers, 1972b; Pohlman, 1971). An incentive in this context is a payment in cash or kind given by an organization to induce birth control. Adopter incentives are those paid directly to an individual or couple, whereas diffuser incentives are given to special change agents who directly or indirectly influence an individual or couple to practice birth control.

CHARACTERISTICS OF INNOVATIONS

We turn our attention now to the various types of innovations and the special attributes of innovations believed to influence their acceptance by organizations. It is not surprising that many classification schemes exist to define the categories of innovations. It is clearly possible to use such classifications as degrees of newness, creativity, and risk; it is also possible to group innovations in terms of the changes they imply, as well as in terms of their costs or utility to the adoption unit or the society. For example, specifically concerned with technological innovations in manufacturing firms, Miller (1971) has noted that (a) such innovations can be process or product oriented; (b) their source can be internal or external to the organization; (c) their main impact can be on the external environment or on the structure and functioning of the enterprise; (d) they can be breakthroughs resulting in a conservation of financial resources; or (e) they can be improvements that do not directly relate to financial resources. In the discussion to follow we examine some of these factors.

Innovation Types

Programmed and Nonprogrammed Innovations. Innovations can be categorized first in terms of their degree of anticipation. Some innovations are programmed; that is, their appearance is scheduled in advance. "There may be creative problem-solving in the creation of the idea, but once it occurs the organization has well defined routines and procedures for evaluating and implementing the idea" (Knight, 1967, p. 484). Extensions of the product line are examples, as was the development of larger jet engines once the decision for jumbo jets was made. The addition of a permanent staff member to perform the functions previously provided by outside consultants is another example.

Some claim (e.g., Knight, 1967), that programmed innovations are relatively uninfluenced by the success or lack of success of the organization. On the other hand, Cooke (1972) has argued that organizational success contributes to the ability of a firm to carry out large-scale programmed product innovations, particularly when the initial payoff of those innovations is well into the future. Organizational success often implies managerial expertise, technological know-how, financial flexibility, and so forth, all of which are necessary for many large, programmed product changes. Although hard evidence is lacking, Knight's position is probably most correct in the instance of small-scale change, whereas Cooke's position clearly concerns large-scale change. Infrequently programmed innovations, at least in the short run and involving only minor or modest change, deal with organization structure.

Nonprogrammed or nonroutine innovations are affected by organizational success. These innovations may be of two general types, slack innovations or distress innovations.

Slack is the difference between the payments required to maintain the organization and the resources obtained from the environ-

ment by the coalition. In general, success tends to breed slack . . .
(therefore) slack provides a source of funds for innovation that would
not be approved in the face of scarcity but that have strong subunit
support (Cyert and March, 1963, pp. 278, 279).

Slack innovations may contribute to the overall technology
of the firm, but they are not adopted as solutions to pressing
company problems. A likely short-run effect of slack innovations is to enhance subunit goals—to increase the status and
prestige of individuals and departments. The search for slack
innovations, according to Knight, is wide and is largely external to the organization, and in the search and selection of
slack innovation care is exercised "not to disturb the internal
structure and operation of the organization" (Knight, 1967, p.
485).

Distress innovation, another form of nonprogrammed innovation, occurs when the organization sees itself as being
unsuccessful. It is stated "that internal changes will occur
rather than changes in products or processes. The company
does not have the excess resources to look outside. It cannot
afford the risk and high cost of introducing a new product or
process and, instead, the company will emphasize cost-reduc-
tion projects" (Knight, 1967, p. 485). Thus under conditions
of stress different kinds of innovation tend to be sought than
under slack conditions. The greater the degree of slack,
Knight hypothesizes, the less predictable and logical the organization's behavior will be. With mild stress, moderate steps
are taken; however, if the moderate steps fail, stress becomes
greater, search becomes more random, and more radical steps
are made in hopes of experiencing a correspondingly radical
improvement in organizational well-being. Cooke (1972),
again somewhat at odds with Knight, argues that Knight
overemphasizes the direction of organizational performance,
equating positive performance with slack and negative performance with distress innovation. Cooke prefers to emphasize magnitude of success more than direction. His magnitude

theory suggests that deviation from the norm is a more powerful predictor of the radicalness of organizational innovation than is the direction of the deviation. Direction may predict the context of the innovation.

A nonprogrammed innovation may also result from a power strategy applied to the adopting agency by another organization. For example, a government agency may stipulate the adoption of a particular innovation as a prerequisite for receiving government funds for the general program of the agency. For instance, the adoption of patient advisory councils by health organizations seems to have been done in compliance with governmental pressure in the form of an implicit threat to withhold federal funds (Bradshaw and Mapp, 1972).

Many of the ideas discussed above are summarized in Figure 1-2. There are two new dimensions, however, in Figure 1-2. The first concerns the categories in which innovations can be grouped or the contexts in which they occur. Product or service innovations and production-process innovations need no elaboration. Organizational-structure innovations, as suggested earlier, may alter the informal social system of the organization, its formal social system, and not infrequently both. Authority structures, formal and informal communication systems, reward systems, and task systems may all be changed. People innovation entails the replacement of old personnel and the addition of new personnel, or it may involve altering the behavior and/or beliefs of organizational members. Radicalness, the degree to which the innovation differs from alternatives including the status quo, is another relevant dimension that is discussed in some detail shortly.

Miller (1971) has noted that in the North American steel industry programmed and nonprogrammed innovations are initiated by different stimuli. Although programmed innovations (such as updating of teaching materials) tend to have as

		Type of Innovation	Radicalness
Successful Organization			
Programed innovation	Style—minor product or service changes, production-process changes, and normal movement of people within the organization	Products and services	Low
		Production process	Low
		Organizational structure	Low
		People	Low
Slack innovation	Wide search—external to the organization—try not to disturb the internal organizational structure	Products and services	Moderate and high
		Production process	Moderate and high
		Organizational structure	Low
		People	Low
Unsuccessful Organization			
Distress innovation — Mild	Internal changes—reduce costs, change organizational structure or reshuffle people	Products and services	Low
		Production process	Low and moderate
		Organizational structure	Moderate
		People	Moderate
— Great	Wide and random search for radical organizational change	Products and services	Low, moderate, and high
		Production process	Moderate
		Organizational structure	High
		People	High
Organization fails			

Figure 1-2. General model of organizational search (From: Knight, 1967).

20

stimuli achievement relative to self-imposed performance goals, nonprogrammed innovations (e.g., instructional simulation games) are initiated by dissatisfaction or accidental encounters with opportunities. From a process point of view, this indicates that the distinction between programmed and nonprogrammed innovations is most relevant as a characteristic during the first major stage of the adoption process, the initiation stage. In general, relatively little is known about slack and distress innovations; further research is required before a more complete understanding is possible.

Instrumental and Ultimate Innovations. In studying social change related to Supreme Court decisions, Grossman (1970, p. 543) makes an important distinction between instrumental innovations and ultimate innovations. The latter are ends in themselves, but the former are aimed at specific changes that are intended, at a later point in time, to make possible or easier the introduction of ultimate innovations. In a university setting the offering of courses not previously taught is sometimes an instrumental innovative act designed to facilitate the eventual establishment of a new department, the ultimate innovation.

A number of considerations are involved here. If we are concerned with planned change, it becomes a strategy decision whether to attempt the ultimate innovation immediately or choose the route of securing the adoption of instrumental innovations. We cannot delve deeply here into the various factors affecting the choice of strategies and tactics, let alone identify the various strategies and tactics available to those concerned with planned intervention in organization (see Zaltman and Duncan, forthcoming). If the change agent, be he a member of the organization or not, has control over substantial desired resources that are scarce to the (other) members of the organization, then a power-coercive strategy could be invoked and the ultimate innovation imposed upon the organization. A power-coercive strategy involves the use and/or threat of force through the application of moral, economic, and political resources to achieve change (Zaltman et al., 1972). If, on the other hand, the change agent has no significant authority or power, he might choose a facilitative strategy in which he secures small-scale changes and provides resources making it easier for the organization to adopt the ultimate innovation (Warwick and Kelman, 1973). The small-scale changes are less threatening and potentially less disruptive innovations but, when aggregated, are quite substantial. Thus the ultimate innovation does not appear too radical when perceived relative to the accumulated instrumental changes. Also, even when an ultimate innovation is generally acceptable at the outset, facilitative or instrumental innovations may still be necessary for effective employment of the ultimate innovation.

Implicit in the notion that instrumental innovation is an element of deliberate intervention in organizations is that knowledge exists concerning what structures or functions should be changed to ease the way for the end innovation. This is not always the case. Knowing what changes in the organization and/or its environment will facilitate other changes in the organization is crucial to this general-change strategy. This information can be very elusive, or at least not readily identified with high degrees of certainty. An understanding of cause-and-effect mechanisms in the structure and functioning of the organization and its interaction with its environment is necessary. Another factor to be considered is the unintended consequences of the instrumental innovations that could have dysfunctional consequences and thereby reduce the adoption probabilities of the ultimate innovation below the likelihood of adoption which existed prior to the introduction of the instrumental innovation(s).

Despite the difficulties associated with pursuing a deliberate strategy of instrumental innovation as a prelude to ultimate innovation, it is an important concept and a practical procedure. It focuses attention on obstacles or resistance to change, which is an understudied area. More importantly, successful instrumental innovation can produce a general climate of innovation, although we hasten to add that a general openness to change is not necessarily an absolute good.

Radicalness—Routine and Innovative Situations-Solutions. Several authors (e.g., Knight, 1967; Harvey and Mills, 1970) have classified innovations in terms of their "radicalness." This notion is closely linked to the now-familiar terms of risk, novelty, and creativity: the more risky and novel the innovation, the more radical it is. Innovation radicalness can be defined in terms of existing alternatives: the more an innovation differs from the existing alternatives, the higher is its degree of radicalness. This definition refers to the situation that the multimember adoption unit faces, which here is called *situation* radicalness; it varies along a routine-innovation continuum. A routine situation is one that the organization has previously experienced, whereas an innovation (radical) situation is completely new. In reference to a theoretical paper by Harvey and Mills (1970), it is indicated later that although there is a tendency for routine situations to be met with routine solutions and for innovative situations to call forth innovative solutions, the initial propensity of an organization to impose routine solutions (perhaps with some adaptation; see March and Simon, 1958) in both types of situations is related to certain identifiable variables. The presence of these variables reduces the units' rate of adoption. Further, when we study the process approach to innovation we shall see that the sequence of process stages for an innovative solution is not the same as in the case of a routine solution.

It is useful to elaborate somewhat more on solution radicalness. If it happens, as indicated above, that innovative situations are met with routine solutions, it is important to distinguish not only between degrees of situation radicalness, but also between degrees of solution radicalness. The definitions of this notion vary among authors. It is sometimes distinguished from *scope*, which may be made operational in terms of the relative number of members of the organization whose behaviors are influenced by the innovation. This seems to be one aspect of Wilson's (1966) definition of innovation: a significant number of tasks concerns the scope of the innovation, whereas a fundamental change might be defined as radicalness. In this book, however, the notion of (solution) radicalness includes scope, which means that the innovations considered influence a considerable number of members of the unit. With this in mind, solution radicalness is defined as the extent to which an implemented (adopted) innovation implies changes in the various subsystems of the organization or in the behavior patterns of its members. A solution-radical innovation is always to some extent disruptive of the *status quo* and involves changes in the subsystems of information, values, incentives, and power, and so on (see, e.g., Littaner et al., 1970, for a case study of innovation in system of feeding infants in hospitals). As in the case of situation radicalness, solution radicalness tends to vary along a routine innovation continuum. A routine solution is one that the organization has used to solve past problems, whereas an innovative (radical) solution is a solution that has not been used before; there are no precedents in the organization for its use (see Harvey and Mills, 1970, pp. 189–190). It should be noted that in many empirical cases, situations and solutions may contain both routine and innovative elements and that qualitative evaluation may have to be used to determine the degree of radicalness. For analytical purposes, however, it is useful to conceptualize each innovation in the above terms. Consider Table 1-2 from Harvey and Mills.

Table 1-3 is a summary of contextual and internal factors describing factors influencing the probable responses (ini-

Table 1-2.   Basic Alternative
Situations and Solutions
Encountered by
Organizations

Problem situation	Solution	
	Routine	Innovative
Routine	A	B
Innovativeness	C	D

(From Harvey and Mills, 1970, p. 190)

tial solution) of an organization in the face of routine and innovation situations. In Chapter 2 behavior of an organization in the face of routine and innovation situations is discussed in more detail.

Some of the changes that a perceived innovative solution imply may be dysfunctional to the organization, that is, they may interfere with the achievement of organizational objectives. Changes present themselves as problematic situations somewhere along the routine-innovation continuum, depending upon the degree to which they are actually perceived as being dysfunctional. In other words, a given innovative *solution* may have dysfunctions that produce new *situations* calling for new and radical (innovative) solutions. For example, a special youth program well-supported with public funds was launched in a large poverty area of a major eastern United States city. The program was originally intended to function in a number of contexts independent of other local organizations. Although the intent was to supplement the activities of these other groups, the real effect was to compete with them. As a consequence, the local organizations were seriously weakened and a number ceased operation. The youth program organization was unable to replace entirely the func-

Table 1.3. Internal and Contextual Variables Affecting the Use of Routine and Innovative Solutions on Both Routine and Innovative Problems

Organizational Variables Affecting Propensity to Impose Particular Solutions on Particular Problems	Tendency to Impose Routine Solutions on Both Types of Problems when:	Tendency to Impose Innovative Solutions on Both Types of Problems when:
Contextual		
Size of organization relative to competitors	Relatively large	Relatively small
Age of organization relative to competitors	Relatively old	Relatively young
Degree of competition in market situation	Relatively uncompetitive market	Relatively competitive
Rate of technological change	Relatively slow	Relatively rapid
Internal		
Diffuseness of organization's technology (size of product line)	Relatively specific	Relatively diffuse
Degree of formalization of internal communication system	Relatively formalized	Relatively unformalized

(From Harvey and Mills, 1970, pp. 190–192)

tions of these local groups, and the general situation in the poverty area deteriorated drastically. The public agency providing primary support for the special youth program subsequently revised its program radically. The new course of action was to contract out all its activities to the local organizations. In this particular context this general strategy was an entirely novel one.

It might be hypothesized that dysfunctional changes occur more frequently the more solution radical the intended changes are. Further, because dysfunctional changes frequently serve as internal stimuli to new innovations, it might also be hypothesized that the higher the degree of solution radicalness of a particular innovation, the more likely it is that a sequence of new solution innovations will emerge in response to the newly created radical or innovative situations. It can be noted that this hypothesized sequence of innovations is unintended, and it should therefore be distinguished analytically from the intended instrumental-ultimate sequence of innovations discussed earlier.

Normann's (1971) analysis of product development in large companies supports the claim that there is utility in distinguishing between innovations along a radical-routine solution continuum. Normann prefers a somewhat different set of terms, however, referring to "variation" that corresponds to routine innovation and "reorientation" that corresponds to radical innovation. A new product is a variation if its "dimensions are basically similar to those of earlier products of the organization, though with refinements and modifications. Reorientations, on the other hand, imply fundamental changes, in which some product dimension may be eliminated and entirely new ones added" (Normann, 1971, p. 205). Clearly, then, of the two types of innovation, reorientation (e.g., team teaching, the use of change teams, and management by grid), is the most radical solution, because it implies major changes in the various subsystems or structural aspects

Table 1-4. Relations of Variations and Reorientations to Organizational Subsystems

Type of Innovation	Type of System		
	Task System	Political System	Cognitive System
Variations	Only minor changes	Accommodated within existing policies and power structures	Existing attention, rules, and heuristics used; direct perception; no change of domain
Reorientations	Basic changes; new types of specialist knowledge and task subsystems needed	New goals, values, and supporting power structures necessary	Change of domain; mediated perception from the secondary environment; existing cognitive structure (attention rules, decision rules, interpretation rules, etc.) insufficient

(From Normann, 1971, p. 207)

of the organization (see Table 1-4). Reorientations also tend to be the most innovative solutions, because there are no precedents for them in the unit—they differ considerably from the solutions that have been implemented (adopted) before. In other words, if a solution is implemented that has not been used before (an innovative solution), changes in the subsystems of the adopting organization are likely to take place (high degree of solution radicalness).

On the assumption that rate of innovation depends upon the degree to which the various subsystems of the organization must be altered, Normann's twofold classification system provides a useful starting base for the development of a classification scheme that can aid in prediction. Given various innovation characteristics, it might be hypothesized that reorientations have a lower rate of adoption than do variations. As Table 1-4 indicates, "variations" (e.g., carpeting patients' rooms, Hepner, 1970) imply only minor changes in the various subsystems of the organization, whereas reorientations imply major changes. For example, new procedures for administering medication in hospitals can alter or create new relationships between engineering and nursing staffs (Coe and Barnhill, 1967). In Robertson's terms (1971), only reorientations have important effects upon established patterns of behavior.

In Table 1-4, Normann suggests that variations (i.e., routine innovations in our earlier terminology) and reorientations (i.e., radical innovations) can have an impact on three types of subsystems within the organization. The first is the task system representing types of specialized knowledge or competence. In the second, the goals, values, and power structure represent the political system. The political system serves as a filter to screen out reorientations that do not fit the power structure. The political system also confers legitimacy that can create consensus leading to the adoption of a radical innovation. The third subsystem is the cognitive system, referring to the "process by which people in the organization get information about the external environment and perceive events in it" (Normann, 1971, p. 206). For example, reorientation may involve the provision of innovations to new markets, thus changing (adding to) the external domain the organization must monitor. The cognitive system also includes internal (to the organization) information processing, although Normann does not emphasize this dimension.

Finally, in reorientations or, again, radical innovations, there appear to be three typical patterns. As distinguished by Normann, these are systematic reorientation, idiosyncratic reorientation, and marginal reorientation. The former are not unlike programmed and instrumental innovations. They are legitimized parts of the organizational development process and are phases in a longer-run orientation. Expanding into new markets and finding areas of application for new technology are examples. Idiosyncratic reorientations are innovations that are not the product of a consistently recurring set of events. They represent the response of someone in a power position who is able to impose change even in the absence of consensus within the organization. A school principal, for instance, may issue a directive that team teaching is to be adopted in specified courses. Marginal reorientations "consist of relatively smaller projects outside the domains (of the organization) which because of their size do not substantially affect the goals and structure of the organization and which are therefore easier to legitimize" (Normann, 1971, p. 210). However, as discussed previously with reference to instrumental innovations, the effect of accumulated marginal innovations can substantially alter the political and cognitive systems of the organization, although this may never have been intended.

Notice that Normann emphasizes what Knight (1967, pp. 482) refers to as performance radical innovations, that is, those innovations which affect the organization's ability to

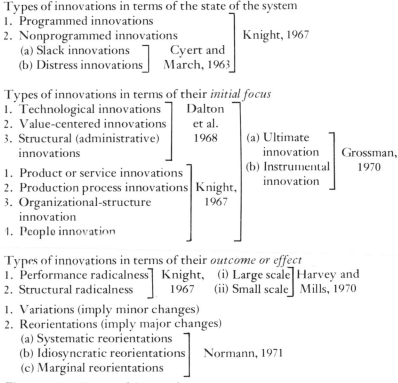

Types of innovations in terms of the state of the system
1. Programmed innovations
2. Nonprogrammed innovations   Knight, 1967
   (a) Slack innovations   Cyert and
   (b) Distress innovations   March, 1963

Types of innovations in terms of their *initial focus*
1. Technological innovations   Dalton
2. Value-centered innovations   et al.
3. Structural (administrative)   1968   (a) Ultimate
   innovations   innovation   Grossman,
1. Product or service innovations   (b) Instrumental   1970
2. Production process innovations Knight,   innovation
3. Organizational-structure   1967
   innovation
4. People innovation

Types of innovations in terms of their *outcome or effect*
1. Performance radicalness   Knight,   (i) Large scale Harvey and
2. Structural radicalness   1967   (ii) Small scale Mills, 1970

1. Variations (imply minor changes)
2. Reorientations (imply major changes)
   (a) Systematic reorientations
   (b) Idiosyncratic reorientations   Normann, 1971
   (c) Marginal reorientations

Figure 1-3. Types of innovations

perform a required task such as meeting a new market demand or new product opportunity. There are, on the other
hand, innovations that are structurally radical; that is, they
are reorientations which change such organizational elements
as communication systems and reward and authority structures. Figure 1-3 summarizes the various types of innovations discussed thus far. It might be noted that Dalton's
(1968) values-centered innovation in Figure 1-3 includes
policy and strategy changes that Knight's classification seems
to exclude. Figure 1-4 presents an alternative way of view-

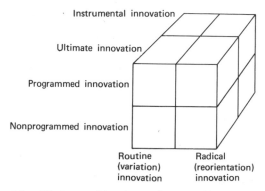

Figure 1-4.   Most likely combinations of types of innovations.

ing the most basic typologies. Thus a given innovation might be instrumental, programmed, and routine. Figure 1-4 implies that the various types are not mutually exclusive, although certain combinations are much more likely to come about than others. Programmed innovations are usually routine innovations, whereas nonprogrammed innovations, particularly the distress variety, often appear as relatively radical innovations because they tend to produce changes in the subsystems of the organization. Depending on the decision-making processes and power relations within an organization, a nonprogrammed innovation may also be an ultimate innovation, particularly if a radical situation exists.

Attributes of Innovations

Thus far we have been concerned with major types of innovations or categories in which they could be placed. Here attention focuses upon attributes that innovations of various types possess and that are known to influence their adoption or rejection. Each of the various types of innovations can possess a varied combination of attributes that have been found to be relevant for describing, explaining, and predicting responses to innovations.

Perhaps the most comprehensive treatment of innovation attributes has been provided by Lin and Zaltman (1973). Much of the discussion in the following paragraphs is adapted from that source.

Cost. Cost is one of the most obvious dimensions. One type of cost is *financial*, which can be divided into (a) initial cost and (b) continuing cost. Initial financial cost, in a study by Fleigel, Kivlin, and Sekhon (1968) of farming enterprises, was found to have a positive partial correlation of plus .43 with the adoption rate when controlling for 14 other attributes. Continuing cost and the adoption rate had a fourteenth-order partial correlation of minus .24. The 14 other attributes studied by these authors are presented in Table 1-5. One explanation is that there is a cost-quality relationship which states that the more expensive an innovation is the higher its quality. The cost might be attributed, in the minds of potential users at least, to a presumed high research-and-development effort. This seems to apply primarily to durable industrial goods that are purchased infrequently and are supposed to have a long life. Thus the perceived extra cost of a particular durable good innovation is, in a psychological sense and in an accounting sense, prorated over a long period of time, which makes the incremental cost (the higher purchase price) appear small.

"The greater the cost in scarce inducements (incentives), the more radical the innovation, regardless of the prospective benefits" (Wilson, 1966, p. 197). The cost of an innovation, Wilson says, is the "extent to which any of these incentives must be redistributed or their supply increased" (p. 197). The incentives can be financial or nonfinancial. Clearly, in this definition radicality of the innovation is seen from the organi-

Table 1-5. Expected and Actual Relationships
between Attributes of Farm Practices
and Rate of Adoption

	Relationships with Rate of Adoption		
Attribute	Expected Direction	Simple Correlation	Partial Correlation
1. Initial cost	−	+.10	+.43
2. Continuing cost	−	+.01	−.24
3. Rate of cost recovery	+	−.10	−.23
4. Payoff	+	+.23	+.36
5. Social approval	+	−.02	+.13
6. Saving of time	+	+.20	+.10
7. Saving of discomfort	+	+.25	+.11
8. Regularity of reward	+	+.14	+.30
9. Divisibility for trial	+	+.36	+.44
10. Complexity	−	−.19	−.00
11. Clarity of results	+	+.07	−.23
12. Compatibility	+	−.23	+.17
13. Association with dairying	+	+.07	+.31
14. Mechanical attraction	+	−.16	−.06
15. Pervasiveness	−	−.28	−.06

(From Fleigl et al., 1968)

zation's point of view, not from the point of view of society. For example, an innovation by a stenographic pool may be more radical than one by a university research team if the cost in inducements for their adoption is higher.

Social cost is another form of expense. Fleigel et al. (1968) found that social cost was an important factor in explaining the rate of adoption in a developing country (an eleventh-order partial correlation equal to plus 46), whereas it was not important in the United States (eleventh-order partial correlation between plus .13 and minus .10). One international management consulting firm observed that even seemingly minor management changes (from the consulting firm's viewpoints) in power or status within the organization, resulting from the adoption of more efficient management science techniques, produced sufficient internal conflict to cause a substantial number of medium-sized business firms in developing areas to discontinue the newly adopted practices. Of course, there is ample evidence in developed nations of what might be classified by an outsider as "overreaction" to modest organizational change (Spicer, 1952).

Social cost may come in the form of ridicule, ostracism, or even exclusion or expulsion from some relevant reference group. Social position within a group influences the degree to which such a cost may occur and how serious the individual may perceive this cost (Homans, 1961). The marginal member of a group may have little to lose by innovating; therefore, even in the presence of considerable disapproval, he may proceed to adopt an innovation. There is always the possibility that the decision might prove to be a wise one, and he may gain stature as a consequence. This is a relatively understudied mechanism whereby innovations enter both formal and informal groups. A high-status member of a group may also adopt, again, even in the presence of potential or actual ridicule. The high-status person can do so because he generally has an inventory of goodwill or social credit upon which he can draw, and he will suffer little if the innovation does not succeed.

Returns to Investment. A second dimension concerns the returns to the investment. This is of special significance among organizations with particularly scarce resources or short-term investment policy preferences. This deferral of gratification varies among firms according to industry and within firms according to type, size of operation, and achievement motivation among management personnel. Return to investment is a more difficult dimension to handle in nonbusiness organizations. For educational innovations, the return-to-investment factor is difficult to determine because the benefits of educational change are often impossible to calculate or define.

Efficiency. Another potentially important factor is the efficiency of an innovation in terms of (a) overall time saving and (b) the avoidance of bottlenecks in particular. In fact, one of the most basic wants acting as a stimulus for change for both individuals and organizations are relief and avoidance wants, that is, the desire to avoid punishment (Barnett, 1953). These represent the desire for nonexistent or not presently possessed means or goals and seem to appear in both industrial and consumer marketing contexts. Time-saving attributes appear to be important in labor-intensive industries, for example, in adoption decisions of moderately small but technically advanced adopters.

Risk and Uncertainty. The risk and uncertainty associated with innovations is also an important factor on which we shall elaborate somewhat more extensively than on other traits. "Where others have innovated, the followers have a much smaller cost of search. Related to this difference is the reduced risk to late adopters where the innovators have demonstrated the possibility of a new idea" (Becker and Whisler, 1963). The relevance of risk varies across social sectors or industries or organizational contexts. Becker (1970) in a study of public health officers has focused on attributes of innovations that emphasize or involve political risk. Among the attributes he considers important are the opportunity for opposition inherent in the proposed innovation and the risk it involves vis-a-vis the officials' reputation or position.

Communicability. The communicability of an innovation exerts considerable influence on whether it is accepted. First, the ease and effectiveness with which the results of the innovation can be disseminated to others constitutes a major force in the diffusion process (Roger and Shoemaker, 1971). This was found to be particularly true with innovations in the United States steel industry (Czepiel, 1972). Linked with this is the *clarity of results* of an innovation. Often innovations are introduced into dynamic situations involving the operation of several factors where there are no effective controls over those other factors. It then becomes difficult to ascribe or attribute to the innovation any changes that may occur after the innovation has been introduced. There is clearly a need for much more work on research techniques in such instances, although some recent advances have already been made (Campbell, 1969). There may also be obstacles (system imposed or otherwise) to communications on innovations. Industry codes of ethics and antitrust laws effectively turn off certain channels of information.

Compatibility. Compatibility concerns the similarity of the innovation to an existing product it may eventually supplement, complement, or replace. Rogers and Shoemaker (1971) present compatibility somewhat differently. They define it as "the degree to which an innovation is perceived as consistent with existing values, past experiences, and needs of the receivers" (p. 145). This assumes that an innovation is perceived in a particular context and that the relationship between the innovation and other elements in that context influence the adoption and diffusion of the innovation. The *pervasiveness* or degree to which an innovation relates to and requires changes or adjustments on the part of other elements in the organization influences the speed of adoption by the organization as a whole and by its constituent members (Menzel, 1960; Linton, 1936; Barnett, 1953). The greater the pervasiveness of an innovation, the slower its acceptance.

The concept of compatibility as a salient attribute of innovations has been most thoroughly reviewed by Thio (1971), who traces its treatment from first use at a cultural level of analysis to a social level. At a social-psychological level of analysis attention has been given to the innovation's "goodness of fit" with such adopter characteristics as personality, emotional attitude, value orientation, previous innovative experience (Brandner and Keal, 1964), beliefs (Yeracaris, 1961), and education and income level (Graham, 1954). The notion of compatability is particularly tied to the psychological-social-cultural world of the potential adopter, and, perhaps more than any other innovation attribute, it must be considered in conjunction with the psychosocial world. Elaborating further, Thio adds two other (in addition to the cultural, social, and social-psychological dimensions) types of adopter-innovation compatability dimensions. Symbolic compatibility refers to the subjective perception of the organization, that is, what an organization sees in the innovation. Functional compatibility concerns what is functionally required of the potential adopter to make use of the innovation. These considerations are raised again in a more organizationally oriented setting in a subsequent part of the book.

Brandner and Keal (1964) tested and found supporting evidence for the proposition that business enterprises (more specifically, the chief decision makers) with an opportunity to evaluate an innovation as congruent with a previously favorably evaluated practice accept the innovation more quickly than those enterprises without this opportunity. However, the more interesting finding is that where congruence is a factor, it is so important that it seems to supersede the significance of factors such as age, educational mobility, economic importance, and other factors normally associated with speed of adoption among organizational personnel.

Complexity. The complexity of the innovation clearly has a bearing on its acceptance. Generally, the more complex an innovation is in terms of operating, the less rapid its acceptance will be. Complexity can become manifest on two levels.

First, the innovation may contain complex ideas. Second, the actual implementation of the innovation may be complex. We might say that an innovation which is easy to use but whose essential idea is complex is more likely to be adopted than an innovation which is difficult to use but whose essential idea or concept is readily understood.

Scientific Status. Another attribute of an innovation that can play an important role in its adoption and diffusion is its *scientific status.* (Havelock, 1970, pp. 8–38, 39). This is as important for new ideas and practices as it is for new products. New knowledge can be an innovation (see, e.g., Zaltman and Koëhler, 1972) in which case its reliability, validity, generality, internal consistency, and so on become important subattributes. It should be added that not all scientifically sound innovations are adopted, nor are all scientifically unsound innovations rejected.

Perceived Relative Advantage. The perceived relative advantage the innovation has over other alternatives, including current practice, is important. Those things the innovation does that other alternatives do not do are its critical attributes. The larger the number of critical attributes and the greater their magnitude, the more likely the innovation is to be adopted. The *visibility* or salience of the relative advantage is important. The more obvious the innovation is, the more likely it is to be adopted. This suggests still another factor. The more amenable to *demonstration* the innovation is, the more visible its advantages are, and thus the more likely it is to be adopted. Demonstration can be viewed in two ways. First, there is "use demonstration" or method demonstration which consists of showing how the innovation is employed. Second, there is "result demonstration" intended to show the benefits of adopting a particular innovation. Ideally it is desirable to be able to conduct both forms of demonstration. Practically speaking, however, this is not often feasible, especially when the innovation is an idea having no physical manifestation. It is not, however, an uncommon practice for a supplier of an innovation to transport entire buying committees to a site where the innovation, for example, heavy machinery, is in actual use.

As previously noted relative advantage has been looked at by some (Knight, 1967) in terms of radicalness instead of relative advantage. Little new is added to our knowledge when only discussing performance radicalness, that is, the amount of change in output that results from one innovation when compared with other alternatives. However, there is still another dimension of innovation radicalness often overlooked (and suggested by Knight, 1967), *structural radicalness*. Structural radicalness occurs when the unique qualities of an innovation bring about alterations in such basic structural elements as communication, authority, and reward systems.

Caution is suggested by one study of several characteristics of innovations (divisibility, communicability, relative advantage, compatibility, complexity) originally summed up by Rogers (1962) that were presented to a panel of educators and administrators. They were asked to rate each of six widespread educational innovations by applying the five characteristics to the six innovations (Carlson, 1968). There was little agreement among panel members in their ratings. This suggests caution in utilizing the various innovation characteristics indiscriminately in different contexts.

Point of Origin. Myers and Marquis (1969, pp. 19–29) in a study of factors underlying industrial innovations in selected firms identify a wide range of innovation characteristics. Their first approach was to classify innovations according to origin: Did it originate within the firm or did the firm adopt it? Interestingly 77% of the innovations studied were originated within the firm. This particular classification factor, point of origin, is important, for it suggests a significant theoretical issue. The salient characteristics of an innovation as seen by the originator need not coincide with those perceived by an adopter or potential adopter. Furthermore, the characteristics of an innovation that are considered important prior to adoption may yield in importance to other factors once the adoption is made and some time has passed. Thus the salient characteristics of innovation may vary according to from whose vantage point it is being perceived and may also vary over time within the viewpoint of any particular observer. Moreover, beyond the adopter-nonadopter dichotomy the innovation may be viewed differently by different ideal-type categories, suggesting that it might be equally profitable to categorize individuals and the organizations to which they belong on the basis of their perceptions of innovations in terms of uniqueness as opposed to or as well as the time they require before adopting.

Myers and Marquis also distinguished between new and modified items where modified was held to be the situation in which the firm was already producing the item affected. Modifications fell into five meaningful categories: improved esthetics, increased utility, increased durability, increased efficiency of performance, and lowered production costs. Approximately two-thirds of the innovations studied were new items. "Almost one-half of the adopted innovations were modifications, compared with less than one-third of the original innovations" (Myers and Marquis, 1969, p. 20). The authors further distinguish between product, component, and process innovations.

Terminality. Terminality is an important but relatively unstudied dimension of many innovations. A terminal represents a specific point in time beyond which the adoption of an innovation becomes less rewarding, useless, or even impossible, such as the installation of innovations in production processes which, if not installed when the plant is under construction, are not likely to be installed until the old innovative equipment is fully depreciated. Many innovations have intrinsic terminals. A new curriculum program is instituted at the start of the school year or not at all. Similarly, a new legislative bill must be acted upon during one session of the legislature or wait until the next session (Walker, 1969); in some instances if it is acted upon and rejected it may require a longer minimum period determined by law before it can come up for adoption again. Some innovations have one or few terminals, whereas others have many. When an innovation has several terminals but the spacing involves long periods of time, they may be seen as having one or few terminals. There is also a tendency on the part of innovation sources to promote adoption by presenting one or few terminal images of the innovation. The number and spacing of teminals may therefore affect the diffusion process drastically.

Status Quo Ante. The degree to which and the ease with which the status quo ante can be reinstated is another factor having a positive relationship with the adoption of an innovation. This characteristic can be termed *reversibility*. Some evidence shows that when a number of alternative innovations are available, the more reversible ones are more likely to be adopted earlier (Taylor, 1970). *Divisibility*, a dimension found in the existing literature, is related to reversibility. The common view of divisibility is the ability to try to implement the innovation on a limited basis. The more limited that basis is, that is, the smaller the amount of resources committed, the more easily the preinnovation *status quo* can be reinstated. Coughlan et al. (1972) distinguish between two types of divisibility. The first reflects the extent to which a complete innovation can be implemented without entirely abandoning current practices. This is exemplified by the adoption of an individualized instruction program in a school. Subjects that readily lend themselves to individualization can be changed over first to provide a trial run prior to individualizing all subject matter taught. The second type of divisibility concerns the extent to which the innovation can be broken down to a set of components that can be implemented gradually with the benefit of feedback.

Commitment. Related to reversibility and divisibility is the degree of commitment required for successful use of the innovation (for a good discussion of the dynamics of commitment see Kiesler, 1971). However, this dimension, in contrast to reversibility and divisibility, involves considerations of attitudinal and behavioral acceptance. Either of these two factors may precede the other. The most favorable condition for adoption and diffusion is when at least a partial behavioral change can precede attitudinal change. First, once a partial commitment has been made, it is more likely to be followed by full commitment than if no prior partial commitment were obtained. Second, there is evidence that even under conditions of involuntary behavioral change attitudes soon become consistent with actual behavior. Furthermore, although it is desirable for the behavioral change to be voluntary, it need not be in order to gain acceptance. Of course, the authority structure of the organization becomes an important factor here. Degree of commitment is relevant primarily in situations where there is considerable participation among organizational members in the decision-making process. A decision to adopt an innovation even if made by only one or a few individuals automatically commits other organizational members to the innovation, in a behavioral context.

Interpersonal Relationships. Another attribute of innovations that has been little studied per se concerns the *impact* of an innovation *on interpersonal relationships* within organizations and between organizations. Certainly many studies have focused on the impact and consequences of an innovation on individuals and groups of various characteristics. But the potential of innovations to have various consequences has received little attention. For example, innovations may vary along a disruptive-integrative continuum. Related to this is the consideration of whether the innovation is more relevant to the socioemotional (internal) functioning of a group than to its task and goal (external) function or vice versa. Is the innovation one whose adoption makes an individual a more (or less) marginal member of the organization? It is quite possible that initial resistance to an innovation by an individual may reinforce or strengthen his relative position in the organization, but as the innovation gains acceptance by others within the organization the nonadopter becomes increasingly marginal (at least in respect to the innovation in question).

Publicness versus Privateness. Publicness versus privateness is yet another dimension and trait of an innovation (Olson, 1971). A public good is one that if it is available to one party in a social system is more or less automatically and simultaneously available to all members of the social system. Fluoridation of a community water system is a public good. Those opposing the concept must accept it. This suggests a related dimension concerning the *size of the decision-making body* required to act on the public good. Can only one person make the decision? Does it require the consent of a simple majority or a smaller or larger number?

Gatekeepers. A related characteristic is the number of "gatekeepers" involved between the introduction of an innovation to an organization and actual adoption of the innovation by the organization. Some innovations require going through a large number of the approval channels before it can be adopted effectively, whereas others do not. Also, there may be a large number of alternative gatekeepers who can introduce an innovation.

Susceptibility to Successive Modification. Susceptibility to successive modifications constitutes still another innovation characteristic. The ability of the innovation, say, a special piece of machinery, to be adapted to improvements in technology as opposed to becoming obsolete because of inflexibility is important. The ability to refine, elaborate, and modify innovations seems particularly important where financial investment is high and the related technology is a rapidly growing one.

Gateway Capacity. Another characteristic concerns the gateway capacity of the innovation. In addition to the intrinsic value derived from the adoption of an innovation, an additional value can accrue to the extent that the *adoption of an innovation can open avenues to the adoption of other innovations.* It could well be that the increased opportunity for the adoption of other innovations is the intrinsic value of the initial facilitating innovation.

Gateway Innovations. In cases where large-scale social change is desired it is fruitful to think in terms of gateway innovations. What constellation of gateway innovations is most likely to bring that change about? Even small changes in the social structure of an organization can have a dramatic impact in the long run by setting the stage for large-scale innovations. After a certain threshold of accumulated adoptions of gateway innovations has been reached, a sudden takeoff may occur. This, of course, has been discussed earlier with instrumental innovations.

Necessity and Sufficiency

One more point should be made. Many attributes commonly associated with innovations are not necessarily related to their being perceived as new. Examples of such attributes are divisibility, communicability, and terminality. Naturally, such factors do not affect the behavior of organizations toward an innovation. Rather, we must distinguish between those factors that are likely to be the components of the innovation and those factors associated with an innovation that function to retard or facilitate its adoption. In addition, there are variables that represent the antecedents of newness. One example is the time with which the potential adopting organization has been exposed to the innovation. Often (but by no means always) this is related to the time an item has been in existence. Only those attributes constituting newness are necessary and sufficient conditions for an idea, practice, or thing to qualify as an innovation. Antecedent variables are necessary but not sufficient; whereas factors, variables, or attributes whose only impact is to influence rate of adoption are neither necessary nor sufficient to make an item an innovation. Two caveats must be mentioned. First, the three categories of attributes shown in Table 1-6 are not mutually exclusive. A given attribute in a given instance could conceivably qualify as an antecedent, newness, or facilitative attribute. Second, the classification of a particular attribute could fall into any one category depending on (1) the context in which the innovation is introduced, (2) the inherent character of the innovation, and (3) the perceptual processes of the potential adopter.

Table 1-6. Necessity and Sufficiency in Innovation-Related Attributes

Antecedent attributes	Newness attributes	Facilitator or inhibitor attributes
Necessary but not sufficient	Necessary and sufficient	Neither necessary nor sufficient

Table 1-7. Attributes of Innovations of Potential Relevance to Each Major Type of Innovation

Attributes of Innovations		
Financial cost	Complexity	Impact on interper-
Social cost	Perceived relative	sonal relationships
Returns to investment	advantages	Publicness
Efficiency	Demonstratability	Number of gate-
Risk and uncertainty	Terminality	keepers
Communicability	Reversibility	Susceptibility to
Clarity of results	Divisibility	successions
Compatibility	Degree of committment	modification
Pervasiveness		Gateway capacity

Table 1-7 summarizes the major attributes of innovations. It might be useful to conclude this chapter with an illustration of some of these dimensions by describing a newly introduced organizational innovation receiving support in the field of education. The innovation in-question is the change-team concept. Stated most generally, this concept entails the designation of two or more individuals within an organization to be responsible for change. It is their task to assist actively in (1) the identification of areas in the organization in need of change, (2) the selection of innovative solutions, and (3) the implementation and follow-through of the solutions.

The change-team concept can be said to be more of a *radical solution* than a *routine solution* because it involves, for the large majority of school organizations, a new structural unit that is charged with a responsibility not previously clearly focused in any existing part of the organization structure. Because responsibility for directed change is diffused throughout the school system, the proposed innovation may appear threatening to many individuals. The concept is wide in *scope* in .that it influences a significant number of tasks within a school system (Wilson, 1966). The change team does not limit its activities to any one area, such as instruction or teacher evaluation; they range across areas. Moreoever, the innocation involves *reorientation* rather than variation (Normann, 1971); that is, it involves basic changes, such as new goals, values, and support structures, and requires new kinds of specialist knowledge. The concept has high *gateway capacity* in that it establishes opportunities for further significant innovations to enter the system. In fact, this feature is the central advantage in the entire argument favoring change teams. It is difficult to determine a priori whether the change-team concept will be *compatible* with the existing system into which it is to be incorporated. There will, of course, be a measure of self-selection involved. School systems with which the idea is compatible will probably tend to adopt innovations more rapidly, and, to that extent, are in less need of this particular innovation; whereas those systems with which the idea is incompatible will tend to resist the idea and probably other innovative ideas as well. The potential for *pervasiveness* is high. The concept, if successfully implemented, may require adjustment or change among many other elements in the social system and perhaps outside, such as parents and developers and suppliers of educational materials. Whether this adjustment is gradual or immediate depends on the strategies employed by the change agents.

The innovation seems to have relatively little *divisibility;* that is, it does not seem to be possible to implement the idea in limited ways that would also permit a fair test of the idea. However, this may be partially a matter of perspective. In a large educational system it may be tried in one or a few of the school districts, in the fashion of a controlled experiment. However, in the experimental groups it would be advisable to employ the concept in full measure.

The innovation will clearly have a strong impact on *social relationships* within the social system in which it is tried. The relative impact it has on the socioemotional functions and the task and goal-related functions remains to be seen. Properly introduced, the concept could well lessen tension by providing a sympathetic ear to members of the system who may feel frustrated or blocked in their efforts to change. The impact on social relationships is an important quality of the innovation that must be considered carefully in both the implementation and evaluation phases. For example, the change team can provide a closed-circuit communication link between the teacher and school principal. Members of the change team would be in direct contact with teachers and principal, thus bypassing assistant principals, department chairmen, and others. One effect would be to give the teacher a feeling of immediacy with the top decision maker. A dysfunctional effect could be the alienation of those people occupying the positions being bypassed. This need not be the case, of course. Change agents could specialize or focus their contacts on a particular group. Thus one agent becomes the contact person for teachers, another for department chairmen, central administration, and so on so that each major part of the school system has its representative.

Another attribute of the innovation is that it is very likely to involve a *collective* rather than individual adoption or rejection process. A number of persons will probably be involved in the decision-making process because of its pervasiveness and impact on social relations. Here again, this is also dependent on the strategy used to implement the concept. Conceivably, the adoption could be brought about by fiat. At the other extreme, adoption could be obtained by achieving a consensus through group discussions. The latter approach will probably be favored in practice. Related to this is the feature of social system nodes or points where the innovation could be introduced into the system. The idea of change team could be put forth by anyone, from the school board to the individual classroom teacher, although the champion of the idea will probably be someone highly placed in the system bureaucracy or someone such as a consultant who is, at least nominally, outside the system.

SUMMARY

This chapter has reviewed several alternative uses of the term *innovation*, indicating that it is used conceptually in different ways. Innovation has been restricted here to mean any idea, practice, or product that is perceived as new by the potential unit of adoption. The desire to adopt or at least to consider adopting an innovation often arises from performance gaps. However, the characteristics of an innovation are important mediating factors between the need and/or desire to adopt an innovation and its actual use. Three basic types of innovations have been identified, and attributes of potential relevance to these innovation types have been reviewed. The attributes of innovations are often management-decision variables, that is, variables management can manipulate or control. For example, the more management can make an innovation divisible, the more it can influence the acceptance of the innovation. The various attributes listed are by no means exhaustive, nor are they all relevant dimensions of all innovations.

2 Processes of Innovation

CONTENTS

Implementation Substage, Individual Resistance Processes, Perception, Motivation, Attitude, Trial, Evaluation, Adoption and Rejection, Resolution.

INTRODUCTION

In this chapter the processes of innovation are discussed in detail, with special emphasis on: (1) decision processes in innovation, (2) stages of the innovation process, (3) control of the innovation process, (4) classes of innovative decisions, and (5) resistance to innovation.

Innovation as a Process

In reviewing some of the fluoridation studies in United States communities, Paul (1961) has indicated that most of the correlations between specified variables and the vote on fluoridation accounts for a relatively low percentage of the variance. Specifically, Paul indicates that

. . . the quest for diagnostic attributes of a fixed nature, whether of communities or of personalities, is approaching a point of diminishing return, and that the course of wisdom lies in directing systematic research attention to the flow of events in a series of particular campaigns (10).

Thus a process approach is used here in discussing innovations in organizations. In the process approach innovation is composed of a set of stages or phases ordered along the temporal dimensions of their anticipated sequence.

The process approach to the study of innovation should be distinguished from the result or the event approach. The

latter of these is an approach in which the result of the innovation, like rate of diffusion or date of adoption, is related to
characteristics of the organization or its members. However,
when looking only at the result of the innovation, both the
decision process involved and the nature of implementation
problems become obscured. Gross et al. (1971) and Ginzberg
and Reilly (1957) have criticized this concept because it treats
innovation as a single event rather than a continually changing process. Rather, innovation should be viewed as involving
an interrelated and complex set of forces that shift over time
(Gross et al., 1971, pp. 30–31). Thus in the process approach, innovation is viewed as an unfolding process consisting of stages in which characteristic factors not only appear
in greater or smaller degree (as in the event approach), but
also in a certain order of occurrence.

DECISION PROCESSES IN INNOVATION

Elements of Decision Making (1)

Decision processes play an important role in innovation because decision makers in the organization are faced with
choices to innovate or not, to select different innovations, to
use different methods of implementation and so on. Decision
making usually involves four steps: (a) the generation of some
subset of alternative courses of action available; (b) a set of
consequences is attached to each alternative; (c) there is some
preference ordering (utility function) in an attempt to rank
the consequences of various alternatives; (d) the decision
makers select the first alternative that meets some minimum
standard of satisfaction with respect to each of the utilities
that are being sought (Taylor, 1965, p. 62). Thus the decision
makers seek an alternative that is good enough—one that
meets some minimal criteria. Decision makers satisfice rather

than maximize in that a satisfactory alternative is sought (Simon, 1957, p. 204; March and Simon, 1958, p. 140).

Uncertain Condition of Innovative Decisions

In making decisions in the innovation process, decision makers may operate under several conditions. They may experience *certainty*, which occurs under rare conditions. Then the decision makers have complete information about the consequences for each alternative. They may also experience *risk*, which occurs when they have accurate knowledge of the probability distribution of the consequences of each alternative (March and Simon, 1958, p. 137). Finally—in the condition most likely to prevail in decision-making concerning innovations—they experience *uncertainty*. Under conditions of uncertainty, they cannot assign probabilities for the occurrence of particular consequences (March and Simon, 1958, p. 137), or at least these probabilities cannot be assigned with any degree of confidence (Duncan, 1972a).

Schon (1967) has emphasized the importance of uncertainty in innovation by indicating that ". . . the innovative work of a corporation consists in converting uncertainty to risk" (p. 25). He then specifies several types of uncertainty in the innovation process. *Technical uncertainty* focuses on the question of whether the innovation is technically feasible (Schon, 1967, p. 26). For example, is it technically feasible to develop a pollution-free gasoline-powered car? At the initial stage of work on these innovations in automobile antipollution devices, it is difficult to identify the types of problems and the resulting difficulty the organization is likely to encounter. Thus there is much uncertainty. There is also uncertainty regarding the *novelty* of the innovation (Schon, 1967, p. 28). What are other organizations doing about this innovation? Each organization cannot be totally certain what other organizations are doing in their development of the innovation.

Each automobile manufacturer may have some knowledge of competitors' development of antipollution devices, but it cannot be certain of their exact nature or of whether these other organizations have already themselves developed the organization's current model and found it unsatisfactory. Finally, there is *marketing* uncertainty (Schon, 1967, p. 29). Once the innovation is developed, can the organization sell it? For example, when style innovations are made in cars, will the public accept these changes? Although market surveys are continually performed, there is always some uncertainty about acceptance of the innovation in the market place.

Performance Gaps and Innovation

The impetus to innovation arises when organizational decision makers perceive that the organization's present course of action is unsatisfactory. When a discrepancy exists between what the organization is doing and what its decision makers believe it ought to be doing, there is a performance gap (Downs, 1966, p. 191). This performance gap increases the search for alternative courses of action. Thus performance gaps provide a stimulus for innovation.

Both March and Simon (1958, pp. 182–184) and Downs (1966, pp. 171–193) have indicated how these performance gaps are determined. The organization's criteria of satisfactory performance, in general, tends over time to adjust to its level of performance achievement (March and Simon, 1958, p. 182). However, there are certain specific ways in which discrepancies between criteria of satisfaction and actual organizational performance can occur, which can then result in a performance gap.

1. The adjustment of the criteria of satisfaction to the level of the organization's performance is slow (March and Simon, 1958, pp. 183). For example, a manufacturing organi-

zation may have high expectations of what its share of the market should be. However, their continued performance may indicate these expectations are too high. There still may be some performance gap as decision makers readjust their expectations downward.

2. Even when the organization is in a stable environment, that is, in a steady state, the criteria of satisfaction, like aspiration levels in general, tend to adjust themselves upward (March and Simon, 1958, p. 183). A manufacturing organization may be producing a product for which there is a relative stable demand from customers. However, over time decision makers may come to believe that the organization could do better in creating a larger demand for its product. Thus expectations for performance have risen in the organization and a performance gap results. The organization's response then is to try and create more demand for its product.

3. There may be changes in the organization's internal environment.

(a) *New personnel* may come into the organization bringing in new expectations concerning what the organization ought to be doing. These new expectations may result in different criteria of satisfaction being developed, which may then result in a performance gap. For example, the Democratic Party in 1972 was radically transformed because of the influx of the young, idealistic, more liberal McGovern delegates.

(b) *Technological changes* may take place within the organization. Changing how people do their jobs can cause resulting changes in the rules and procedures operating in the organization and the way people interact, which can then create new performance gaps. For example, the introduction of a new management information system in an organization may be promoted as increasing the information gathering and processing capabilities of the organization. Once the new system becomes operational, organizational personnel will expect the system to be more efficient than previous systems. If, for some reason, the new system does not initially exceed past performance, a performance gap will result. The new system is not as effecient as it "ought to be".

(c) There may be *shifts in the power relationships* between individuals and groups in the organization. Groups may change their preferences for certain outcomes, with the result that their criteria for satisfactory performance may change, which may then result in a performance gap. For example, with the advent of police unions, police personnel now expect the regularization and legalization of the discipline process within the police department, which reduces the arbitrary control of the chief (Juris and Feiulle, 1973).

4. There may be changes in the organization's external environment.

(a) The market of importance for the organization's *output* may have changed. For example, if there is no longer a demand for the organization's output, the organization will definitely perceive a performance gap and will initiate a search for a new output to be developed. For example, when the new polio vaccine was developed, the March of Dimes was forced to change their operation to focus on satisfying a different output of working on reducing birth defects (Sills, 1957).

(b) There may be *technological changes in the larger environment* that may change organizational members' criteria of performance satisfaction (Downs, 1966, p. 172). The development of new management information systems create higher expectations on the part of many managers with regard to how their particular organization "ought to" gather and process information. The result is a performance gap that stimulates the search for management information systems for the organization that can be implemented.

(c) There may be *changes in the organization's power position* in relation to other organizations in the environment.

During the early 1960s, universities were in a relatively favorable power position within their environment. They received generally favorable support, both morally and financially, from other institutions and groups in society. However, during the campus demonstrations and riots of the late 1960s, universities came under increasing criticisms. They lost both moral and financial support from many segments of society. Many universities had to reassess what they ought to be doing. The result was that many fringe programs were cut back or dropped.

Thus an important impetus to innovation in organizations is the awareness on the part of organizational decision makers that there is, in fact, some performance gap. This gap then produces the search for alternative courses of action. In conceptualizing innovation as a process of temporally linked stages, the first subprocess is initiation, which is a response to a performance gap. These various stages of the innovation process are discussed next.

STAGES OF THE INNOVATION PROCESS

At the outset, it is useful to subdivide the innovation process. From the point of view of the individual adoption unit, the two resulting stages can be termed "initiation" and "implementation." Most diffusion theorists generally terminate their analysis at the stage of initiation, that is, at the point either where the new idea has become legitimated by powerholders of the unit or where the decision has been made to implement the new idea. What must be done, thereafter, in terms of actually implementing the idea—of actually changing the unit, its subsystems, or the behavior of members—is not considered or is important only to the extent it has influence upon the decision to "initiate" the innovation. An example of

this type of study is that by Walker (1969). In studying diffusion of innovation among the United States, he focused on
". . . one of the most fundamental policy decisions of all:
whether to initiate a program in the first place" (p. 880). In
defining an innovation as a program or policy that is new to
the states adopting it, he considers "adoption" to have taken
place when a program or policy has become enacted by the
state legislature. The implementation of specific programs or
policies in a state is not considered, however, as his following
example from Oklahoma clearly indicates: "Oklahoma's legislature . . . emulated other states by creating a state civil
rights commission, but once the commission was established,
only $2500 was appropriated for its operation" (p. 882).
Whatever happened to this civil rights commission is outside
the scope of Walker's study; the innovation is "adopted"
when a specified decision has been made.

On the other hand, the stage of implementation, the actual mechanics of managing the changes that innovation may
imply, has been the subject of another large body of literature. In this case, the writers have assumed that initiation has
taken place and that the new idea has been made legitimate
by the unit's power center(s), or that the decision for implementation has been made. Much of the literature on organizational change falls into this category, as does the literature on
planned change or "deliberate innovation" (Bennis, 1966;
Hornstein et al., 1971). It appears, then, that the studies of
diffusion of innovations and the studies of planned or managed change tend to focus on two different stages of the same
process. As noted by Becker and Whisler (1967), ". . . the
theory of (diffusion of) innovation, when adequately developed, will complement the 'theories' of 'managed change' (p.
466).

During recent years, most theorists who apply the process approach to the study of innovation with respect to multimember adopter units have conceptualized the stage of "ini-

tiation" in terms of problem solving or decision making. March and Simon (1958) take as their starting point what is known as the problem-solving process at the individual level, then introduce organizational considerations. Both Miller (1971) and Utterback (1971b) think that "initiation" in manufacturing firms is composed of a set of decision-making stages. Kelley and Thibaut (1969) have focused specifically on problem solving in small groups, and Straus (1970) has taken the same approach with respect to families. Walker (1969) applies the theories of organizational decision making in order to find the answers to specific questions related to rate of adoption and diffusion of innovations in the United States. Similarly, taking a diffusion research viewpoint, Rogers and Shoemaker (1971) analyze the decision-making process in communities and the roles played by different individuals as this process unfolds.

Figures 2-1 and 2-2 summarize some of the various models of the innovation process. Figure 2-1 provides a summary of the individually oriented, more micromodels as most completely specified by the Robertson (1961) and Zaltman and Brooker (1971) models. Figure 2-2 provides a summary of the organizational model as represented by our model. Thus as specified in our model in Figure 2-2, the process of innovation may be seen as composed of two major stages with three and two respective substages.

Initiation Stage

Knowledge-Awareness Substage. If an innovation is viewed as ". . . any idea, practice, or material artifact perceived to be new by the relevant unit of adoption" (Zaltman and Lin, 1971, pp. 656–657), then knowledge of the innovation is a crucial first substage of initiation. Thus before any innovation can take place or be adopted, potential adopters must be

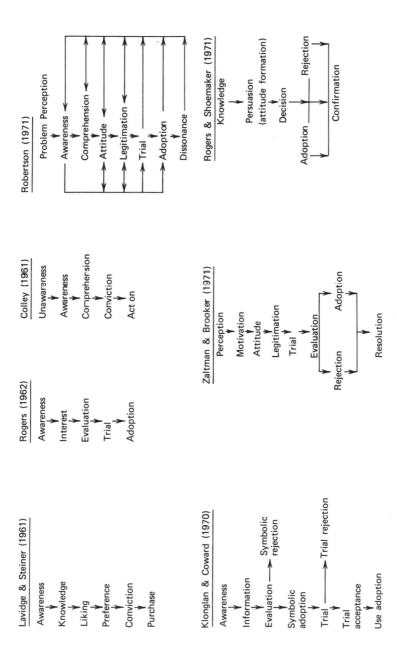

Figure 2-1. Summary of individual-oriented models of the innovation process.

Milo (1971)	Shepard (1967, p. 470)	Hage and Aiken (1970, p. 113)
1. Conceptualization	1. Idea generation	1. Evaluation
2. Tentative Adoption	2. Adoption	2. Initiation
3. Resource Getting	3. Implementation	3. Implementation
4. Implementation		4. Routinization
5. Institutionalization		

Wilson (1966)	Zaltman, Duncan and Holbek
1. Conception of the Change	I. Initiation stage
2. Proposing of change	1. Knowledge-awareness substage
3. Adoption and Implementation	2. Formation of attitudes toward the innovation substage
	3. Decision substage
	II. Implementation stage
	1. Initial implementation substage
	2. Continued-sustained implementation substage

Figure 2-2. Summary of organizational oriented models of the innovation process

aware that the innovation exists and that there is an opportunity to utilize the innovation in the organization.

A major question here is whether the awareness or knowledge of the innovation comes first, followed by the development of a need to innovate or vice-versa. Does the awareness of an innovation stimulate a need to adopt it, or rather does a particular need that the organization has increase the search processes with the result that more awareness of their potential innovations is increased? Rogers and Shoemaker (1971) in their comprehensive analysis of innovations conclude that

. . . research does not provide a clear answer to this question of whether awareness of a need or awareness of an innovation (that creates a need) comes first. The need for some innovations, such as a pesticide to treat a new crop pest, probably comes first. But for other new ideas, the innovation may create the need (p. 106).

Our earlier discussion of performance gaps might provide some insight into this need versus knowledge-awareness issue. When organizational decision makers perceive that there is a discrepancy between criteria of satisfactory performance (what they ought to be doing) and their actual performance, search for alternative courses of action is likely to increase. This increased search is then likely to facilitate the perception and resulting awareness of new innovations that might be adopted. For example, a firm's competitive position may be declining with the result that it increases its search for new product areas it might enter. This increased search is likely to bring the organization in contact with product innovations it might consider.

On the other hand, awareness of an innovation that would markedly improve the organization's functioning, either internally or in its relationship with the outside environment, may alter the frame of reference held by decision makers. This could lead to the perception of a performance gap, whereas prior to awareness there was no gap. For example, a data-processing department in an organization may believe, based on its own performance criteria and the feedback from its users within the organization, that its capabilities and performance are very good. However, in sending its personnel to data-processing conventions, they may become aware of new machines and software that could significantly improve their capacity. This awareness of these innovations can lead to a performance gap in that the data-processing personnel change their expectations concerning what their performance should be.

Formation of Attitudes Toward the Innovation Substage. In this substage, organizational members form attitudes toward the innovation (Zaltman and Brooker, 1971; Rogers and Shoemaker, 1971). Once search has taken place and there is some motivation to change, the attitudes organizational members have toward an innovation are important. There are at least two important attitudinal dimensions that organizational members can exhibit about the innovation (Duncan, 1972b). First, is *openness to the innovation.* Important components of openness to innovation are (1) whether organizational members are willing to consider the innovation, (2) whether they are skeptical about the innovation, (3) whether they feel the innovation will improve how the organization carries out its function. The second important attitudinal dimension is organization members' perception of *potential for innovation.* This attitudinal dimension focuses on whether organizational members perceive that (1) there is some capability within the organization for utilizing the innovation, (2) the organization has had some success in the past in utilizing innovations, (3) there is some commitment on the part of organizational members to working for the innovation and dealing with some of the potential problems that might arise as implementation is attemped.

In considering the effect of attitudes on the innovation process, it is also necessary to consider the overt behavior demanded by the formal organization (2). When there is ". . . . (a) descrepancy between an individual's attitude toward an innovation and the overt behavior (adoption or rejection) demanded by the decision unit" (Rogers and Shoemaker, 1971, p. 31) innovation dissonance occurs (see Festinger, 1957). From Table 2-1, it can be seen that there are two kinds of innovation dissonance. The dissonant adopter is where the individual's attitude toward the organization is unfavorable, but the organization demands overt adoption. The dissonant

Table 2-1.   Four Dissonant-Consonant Types
on the Basis of Individual Attitudes
Toward an Innovation and the Overt
Behavior Demanded by
the Organization

Member's Attitude Toward the Innovation	Overt Behavior Demanded by the Formal Organization		
	Rejection		Adoption
Unfavorable	I Consonant rejector	←	II Dissonant adopter
	↑		↓
Favorable	III Dissonant rejector	→	IV Consonant adopter

(From Rogers and Shoemaker, 1971, p. 31)

SOURCE: Adapted from Knowlton (1965, p. 53), and used by permission.
Note that the arrows in the table indicate pressures toward consonance.

rejector is where the individual's attitude toward the innovation is favorable, but the organization demands overt rejection of the innovation. (Rogers and Shoemaker, 1971, p. 31) Rogers and Shoemaker (1971) indicate that over time this dissonance is reduced by

. . . (1) individuals changing their attitudes to make them consonant with the behavior demanded by the organization, or (2) discontinue the innovation, misuse the innovation, or circumvent the adoption edict to make their organizational behavior consonant with their attitudes (Rogers and Shoemaker 1971, p. 311).

Mohr's (1969) work in health organizations has also indicated that the role of attitudes toward the innovation should not be overemphasized in excluding other variables. He points out that the willingness to innovate may lead to innovation only when individuals involved are not only willing to innovate, but also are strongly impelled and when the resources for innovation are available (Mohr, 1969, p. 117). In studying innovation in 29 health departments, Mohr found that "When resources are high . . . a unit increase in health officer motivation . . . has about 4½ times the effect upon innovation, as it does when resources are low" (Mohr, 1969, p. 124). Thus Mohr concludes that it is necessary to consider the interaction between the variables of motivation to innovate and resources available in predicting innovation (Mohr, 1969, p. 124).

Decision Substage. In this substage, the information concerning the potential innovation is evaluated. If organizational decision makers are highly motivated to innovate and/or their attitudes are favorable regarding the innovation, there is likely to be a favorable attitude to implement the innovation. On the other hand, if there is not much motivation to innovate and/or the attitudes toward the innovation are not favorable, there is a greater liklihood that the innovation will not be implemented.

Thus at this point in the innovation process, the organization needs to process a good deal of information. It is therefore necessary for the organization to have effective channels of communication. In Chapter 3 we discuss the characteristics of organizations as they affect the innovation process, focusing specifically on factors affecting the organization's information gathering and processing capabilities.

Implementation Stage

This second major stage of the innovation process is concerned with the actual utilization of the innovation by organizational members as they perform their tasks. There are two substages in implementation.

Initial Implementation Substage. In this substage, the organization makes the first attempt to utilize the particular innovation. For example, organizations, after deciding to implement management science techniques, often implement them on a trial basis to determine if they are practical before a commitment is made to the establishment of a full-time department. Thus this substage involves some trial of the potential adoption (see Bean, 1972; Radnor et al., 1968; Radnor et al., 1970).

Continued-Sustained Implementation Substage. If the initial implementation has been successful in that organizational members understand it, have information about implementation, and experienced few significant problems (Achilladelis et al., 1971), there is a greater likelihood that the innovation will be continued to be implemented.

Although many theorists agree upon the sequencing of subphases in the "initiation" stage (see Figure 2-1), there is less agreement in the literature concerning the more specific conceptualization of the "implementation" stage. Frequently, theorists do not specify any subphases that are expected to occur in a temporal sequence but simply talk in terms of "realization" or "execution of the new idea." Exceptions here are some intervention theorists and practitioners (Schein, 1969; Lippitt, Watson and Westley, 1958; Beckhard, 1969) of managed or planned change who have developed several approaches to implementation of innovation. Within these approaches, sequences of phases have been proposed, which are usually defined in terms of specific behaviors or tasks. Figure 2-3 presents a summary of some of the tasks of the change-agent interventionist as specified by several theorists.

It appears, however, that one problem with some of these sequences is that they have been developed from case studies without much of a theoretical base. Though rich in

Lippitt et al. (1958, pp. 91–125)	Argyris (1970, pp. 16–31)	Beckhard (1959, pp. 15–19)	Kahneman and Schild (1966, p. 73)
1. Diagnosis of problem	1. Generation of valid information within client system	1. Initial contact by client system	1. Determine whose behavior is to be changed
2. Assessment of client systems motivation and capacity to change	2. Generation of free and informed choice on part of organizational members in affairs of organization	2. Defining the problem and establishing the relationship	2. Determining what groups and individuals are likely to play roles in resistance or change processes
3. Assessment of change agent's motivation and resources	3. Helping client system members develop internal commitment to change process	3. Planning first action step	3. Determine for each key person what are the determinants of his response to change
4. Selecting appropriate change objectives		4. Assessment of effects	4. Determine structure of personal influence in change target system
5. Choosing appropriate helping role		5. Replanning and re-establishing the relationship	5. Determine for each individual in system what can reduce resisting forces and increase forces for change
6. Establishing and maintaining of relationship with the client system			6. Reevaluation of whether change can be obtained within reasonable time and cost
7. Recognizing and guiding the phases of change			
8. Choosing appropriate specific techniques and modes of behavior			

Figure 2-3. Change agent-interventionist tasks as specified by change theorists

insight, they cannot easily be applied to multimember adoption units in general. Case studies of particular multimember units often tend to emphasize the uniqueness of each unit and the particular way its members deal with an innovation. Cross-unit comparisons, however, require the development of a conceptual approach that is simple enough to make use of the "unique" data and at the same time detailed enough to assist in the formulation of hypotheses for research. The problem-solving approach of the "initiation" stage seems to fulfill this requirement quite well. As far as the "implementation" stage is concerned, however, the matters are complicated by the fact that a multitude of possible "strategies" exist (T-groups, group decision making, etc.) even within the specific approaches that focus on the individual (see Beckhard, 1969).

Discussing interventions from the point of view of process consultation, Schein (1969) arrives at much the same conclusion as do the authors who have noted the difficulties of choosing between a multitude of possible strategies:

> . . . one cannot specify particular recipes for intervention or particular sequences which should be used in any given project. A sequence which may work in Company A may well be all wrong in Company B. Instead, the consultant must be ready to intervene in a variety of ways as opportunities arise and as his judgement tells him certain actions are appropriate (Schein, 1969, p. 122).

The present state of the art of intervention theory does not allow for a clear-cut sequencing of phases during the stage of "implementation", because such a sequence varies with the strategy chosen and because few objective "rules" exist for choosing between strategies (3).

A multitude of proposals for sequences through the major stage of "implementation" exist. Few, if any, seem to be applicable to multimember adoption units in general, for reasons indicated above. Schein's (1969) three-step sequence of "action planning," "action steps," and "evaluating outcomes" seems to be too general for comparative purposes. The same objection can indeed be voiced against the two-step sequence chosen in this paper: "initial implementation" and "continued implementation." However, as will be indicated in Chapter 3, different variables seem to be important for these two stages.

It should be emphasized that although the sequence in Figure 2-2 is what might be expected, it is by no means presented as a necessary or invariant order of events. A "beginning" and "end" have been assigned to the innovative process in the form of the arising of a problem situation and the implementation of a solution (an innovation). This is done for analytical purposes. In reality, however, the process of innovation is probably "circular" in that each solution or outcome of the process "feeds back" into the adoption unit in the form of new problems (perceptions) which require attention. For example, as the organization moves to the implementation stages and actually begins to integrate the innovation into its ongoing operation, it increases its knowledge and awareness of the innovation. It may be that not until the organization actually tries to use the innovation does it truly become aware of all its ramifications. At this point then some unanticipated problems may arise.

CONTROL OF THE INNOVATION PROCESS

Feedback and Innovation

Schein's (1970) adaptive-coping cycle emphasizes the importance of feedback in explaining how organizations adapt to their internal and external environments. Specifically the adoptive-coping cycle has six stages:

1. Sensing a change in some part of the internal or external environment.

2. Importing the relevant information about the change into those parts of the organization that can act upon it.

3. Changing production or conversion processes inside the organization according to the information obtained.

4. Stabilizing internal changes while reducing or managing undesired by-products (undesired changes in related systems which have resulted from the desired changes).

5. Exporting new products, services, and so on, which are more in line with the originally perceived changes in the environment.

6. Obtaining feedback on the success of the change through further sensing of the state of the external environment and the degree of integration of the internal environment (Schein, 1970, p. 120).

These six stages are somewhat comparable to those presented in our model of innovation process in Figure 2-2. The first two stages in Schein's cycle are related to initiation, whereas the next four stages are related to implementation (the decision arrived at is apparently made between stages 2 and 3). Schein's last stage in the "adaptive-coping cycle" concerns the obtaining of feedback on the success of change. This creates the "circularity" of the process. However, in the present discussion, feedback is not treated as a stage of its own. Rather, in many organizations feedback often occurs at a multitude of the substages specified in Figure 2-2, thereby creating "circularity" not only for the process as a whole, but for smaller subprocesses as well. Feedback serves the purpose of guiding and controlling the actual performance of a process, and is treated in the following section on control of innovation processes.

The first major stage of initiation, consisting of substages of problem solving, is an iterative process. This means that the decision maker or decision-making group returns to previous substages, then goes through the following steps in a new round. The length of time this feedback takes to return to previous stages depends on the time and resources available, the type of problem considered, and the expected radicalness and quality of solution.

When there are little time and few resources, decision

making becomes more rapid. For instance, in a crisis situation the rate of sequencing through the initiation stages must be high if the solution or innovation to be arrived at is to be of any use to the organization. In studying crisis in organizations, Herman (1963) has indicated that, as crisis increases, the number of communication channels used in the collection and distrubution of information is reduced. This can be counterproductive to the organization because decision makers then have less information about alternative courses of action that might facilitate innovation.

On the other side, conscious feedback returns during the first major stage of initiation and accompanying slowdown in speed of problem solving may take place, if serious behavioral and technical problems are *expected* to emerge during the second major stage of implementation. For instance, if it appears necessary (in a problematic situation) to introduce an innovation of the reorientation type, the decision maker's anticipation of new emerging problems, because of a high degree of solution radicalness, is likely to make him more cautious to slow down the sequencing through the decision substage favorable feedback returns to previous phases before the final decision is made.

In general, control of actual decision-making performance (by means of feedback) during the stage of initiation has an important twofold purpose. First, conscious control at this stage makes possible a specification of means that can be used to control *expected* performance at the next major stage of implementation. Second, careful considerations as the process of decision making unfolds make possible the creation of functional feedback mechanisms that can be used to control *actual* implementation performance. Feedback information makes possible the guidance of actual implementation and behavior changes and may indicate needs for new innovation and change.

A carefully made innovation decision is arrived at in

view of the problems that implementation is expected to imply. However, a decision can seldom be made that avoids all implementation problems in advance. In the case of a solution-radical innovation, some new problems will always emerge, and among these some may be completely unanticipated. To cope with both anticipated and unanticipated problems, it is important and indeed necessary to apply feedback mechanisms that can provide information as to when and where the problems emerge. This information must further be interpreted in terms of the consequences that the emerging problems are likely to have for the organization as a whole. Mann's (1957) feedback of survey results as a basis for change is a good example. This process involves the systematic collection of data concerning organizational problems. Once the data are collected they are fed back to the relevant units in the organization where planning for change is then carried out.

Some of the emerging problems may be serious in the sense that they are clearly dysfunctional to the organization. This means that the innovative solution originally arrived at may have dysfunctions that appear as more-or-less innovative situations, requiring new problem solving. The very first substage of the initiation process is issue perception, which means that the problems occuring because of the implementation of an innovation must be *perceived* as problems to induce (innovative) problem solving. Issue perception may be related either to external or internal stimuli. Accordingly, one can distinguish between two kinds of feedback, which may provide externally or internally generated information, respectively.

Katz and Kahn (1966) have pointed out that most organizations have feedback from the environment, that is, *externally* generated feedback. This is essentially a situation similar to that which may have caused the organization to introduce the innovation in the first place, say, at the time T-1. At a later point in time, T-2 feedback may be obtained from the environment to evaluate whether the innovation was a success. This feedback can be from the reception of the organization's product by the clientele or market (Katz and Kahn, 1966, p. 416).

Many organizations also obtain feedback from their own internal functioning, that is, *internally* generated feedback. In this case, Katz and Kahn (1966) distinguish between feedback that concerns the technical side of internal functioning and feedback that conerns the human (social) side. In terms of the presently applied notion of "subsystem," these two types of internally generated feedback refer to the technical and social "subsystem," respectively.

There may be various types of feedback that occur. Stufflebaum (1967, pp. 129–131) has noted several types of evaluation or feedback processes when discussing evaluation of change in educational systems. *Context* evaluation or feedback involves the continual monitoring of the system to determine unmet needs and the underlying causes of problems. *Input* evaluation or feedback concerns the assessment of possible solutions and alternatives for alleviating system needs as they are proposed by organizations or individuals outside the system. Once an innovation is selected, *process* evaluation or feedback can occur to determine whether the innovation is working as expected and to identify any modifications that might be required. *Product* evaluation or feedback focuses on the measurement of the innovation's overall quality and effectiveness in meeting the system's needs.

Whether an organization generates information related to the technical or social side of its internal functioning is likely to vary with type of organization considered. Although many voluntary organizations emphasize feedback related to the social aspects, economic organizations often are primarily concerned with the technical side of internal functioning. Such emphasis upon a specific subsystem as the source of the internally generated information may often be unfortunate for the organization as a whole in that feedback from other subsystems typically reaches the upper echelons only when some problem has become acute. Although the sociotechnical approach has demonstrated that problems related to the social side of the organization's functioning frequently show up in its technical functioning, technical deficiencies cannot always be adequately explained and coped with unless feedback from the social system is established and corresponding information interpreted. Similarly, emerging deficiencies related to the social system often require feedback from the technical system.

An Example of the Feedback Process in Innovation

An illustrative example, emphasizing the importance of anticipating implementation problems in advance and especially of obtaining internally generated feedback information, is provided by Gross et al. (1971). When studying an unsuccessful educational innovation in an elementary school, these authors identify two fundamental deficiencies in the strategy used by the decision maker (school director). First, the strategy ". . . failed to identify and bring into the open the various types of difficulties teachers were likely to encounter in their implementation attempts" (p. 194). In other terms, the innovation decision was not arrived at in view of the implementation problems that were most likely to emerge. If potential implementation problems had been anticipated during the initiation stage, one might assume that efforts could have been instituted prior to the implementation of the innovation, thus removing or at least minimizing, in advance, the impact of some of the emerging problems and difficulties.

The second deficiency identified was that the decision-maker's strategy ". . . failed to establish and use feedback mechanisms to uncover the barriers that arose during the period of attempted implementation" (Gross, et al., 1971, p. 184). The "barriers" refer to a number of obstacles that the organization members (teachers) actually encountered when they attempted to carry out the innovation. The following barriers were identified: lack of clarity about the new role performance, lack of skills and knowledge, unavailability of required materials and equipment, and certain organizational arrangements. Although the first two may be classified as barriers characterizing individuals or subunits in the organization, the latter is a barrier that characterizes the organization as a unit (4). Even if potential implementation problems had not been anticipated during the initiation stage, feedback mechanisms might have uncovered the barriers to the decision maker and given him the information needed to minimize their impact. In the case reported by Gross et al., however, feedback mechanisms were not created:

> . . . even when limited opportunities were provided for teachers to inform administrators about their difficulties, such as faculty meetings, management failed to provide an atmosphere which invited and allowed teachers to speak frankly (p. 210).

The administrators of the school were not aware of the importance of anticipating the problems that might occur during the change efforts, nor did they create feedback mechanisms that could ensure that problems being encountered were aired and heard. These two strategy deficiencies were, according to Gross et al., the main reasons why implementation was blocked by teachers, despite an initially favorable attitude toward the innovation among this group of organization members.

The lack of feedback considered by Gross et al. (1971) was the internally generated type of feedback. Since the organization studied was a school, externally generated feedback might eventually have been considered in terms of, say, information obtained from parents of the schoolchildren. Further, if the innovation had become a success, feedback might in the longer run have been externally generated in terms of some proficiency evaluation of the children by other organizations in the school's environment.

The Nature of Innovation Processes and Feedback

Generally speaking, it is important to note that although the creation of feedback mechanisms is a prerequisite for adequate handling of emerging implementation problems, it is not in itself a "safeguard" assuring such handling. The information that the feedback mechanisms provide must be interpreted to become useful. But as Elbing (1970) has noted, the meaning of incoming information can be clear cut only if its context has been structured in a clear-cut way. It is of utmost importance, therefore, to formulate explicit problem statements as well as explicit solution plans for implementing the innovation. Explicitness in every subphase of the innovation process is necessary to provide clear bases for the assessment of feedback.

The formulation of explicit problem statements and solution plans is not a task to be performed only with respect to the innovation originally considered and implemented. Because every implementation step may in some way alter the problem situation, it is of vital importance to distinguish between the original problem situation to which a response was made and the problem situation at any later point in time. For example, an organization may need to make a product innovation to meet competitive pressures (the original problem situation). However, as the product innovation is developed and is ready to be implemented into the organization's production, a new problem situation may arise when engineering difficulties are experienced. Thus a new problem situation is experienced in the implementation stage that may require additional engineering innovation. The problem situation now has been altered from simply developing a new product innovation to one of also making certain engineering innovations that may facilitate clearly the original problem situation. Thus it may be that the engineering problems experienced in the implementation stage may redefine the original product innovation.

It can be hypothesized that the more solution radical the innovation, the more likely problems will emerge in the process of implementation. Accordingly, the more solution radical the innovation, the more important it is to create feedback mechanisms that can identify and deal effectively with these emerging problems. Because problems can emerge at any point in time, evaluation of feedback information should take place rather frequently. Elbing (1970) has emphasized that each step during the major stage of implementation should be performed ". . . on the basis of a combining assessment of feedback or responses from the preceding step" (p. 317). In terms of the two subphases of implementation applied here, this would mean that after an "initial implementation" (subphase), the implications of "subsystem" and behavior changes should be assessed to determine how to perform "continued/sustained" implementation (subphase 5). However, to provide a basis for feedback assessment which is structured in a clear cut and explicit manner, these two general subphases of implementation must be broken down into more detailed steps for each specific innovation.

CLASSES OF INNOVATIVE DECISIONS

The central aspect of the innovation classification is the degree to which an innovation necessitates specific changes in the organization. The changes considered usually occur only after the implementation decision has been made; that is, the changes occur during the second major stage of the innovation process. This does not mean, however, that type and radicalness of the changes are of importance only during the implementation stage. The rate of sequencing through the various subphases of the initiation stage to a great extent depend upon both the anticipated consequences of implementation and the class of innovation decision that is made.

Table 2-3.   Steps in Authority and Collective Innovation Decisions

Authority Innovation Decisions	Collective Innovation Decisions
1. Knowledge	1. Stimulation
2. Persuasion	2. Initiation
3. Decision	3. Legitimation
4. Communication	4. Decision
5. Action	5. Action

(From Rogers and Shoemaker, 1971, p. 306)

Two major classes of innovation decisions in organizations are considered briefly: (1) authority decisions and (2) collective decisions (Table 2-3). The basis of categorization as it is viewed here is the degree to which members of the unit can participate in the various subphases of the major stage of initiation. Although authority decisions (without participative management) are made by an individual or by a small group that is often called the "dominant coalition" (Thompson, 1967), collective decisions are made by all or a majority of the adoption unit's members. This means that for collective decisions, political processes are at work during the decision subphases of initiation. Here the choice between alternatives (including the implementation decision) is basically a question of winning approval for an alternative, which involves political processes of conflict and bargaining (Wilson, 1966). For authority decisions, on the other hand, the conflicts occur mainly during the implementation stage and often involve resistance to change. It is important to note that a dominant coalition of say, a profit organization may often make a collective decision. However, from the point of view of the organization as a whole and the majority of its members, this decision is an authority decision in that it is initiated at and controlled from the top of the organizational hierarchy.

Authority Decisions

Thus in authority decisions, the innovation decision is forced upon the members of the adoption unit by someone in superordinate power position (Rogers and Shoemaker, 1971). It appears useful and indeed important to distinguish between two types of authority decisions, both of which are more common in formal organizations (and some small groups) than in other types of adoption units: (a) authority decisions with member participation (the participative approach) and (b) authority decisions without member participation (the authoritative approach). An example of an authoritative approach is the unilateral decision on the part of a manufacturing foreman to request that his personnel begin to use a new assembly process. A participative approach is for the foreman to involve his personnel in the decision on how the new assembly process is to be implemented. This procedure might then reduce some of the resistance to the change. Thus in the participative approach, there is a wider sharing of power; the decision to implement the innovation is ultimately made by the persons in power positions, but it is done in consultation with those affected by the change.

Decision by authority is usually regarded as efficient because the sequencing through the subphases of the initiation stage, and thus the implementation decision, can be made within a relatively short period of time. Many authors emphasize this point, especially for authority decisions without member participation. For instance, Rogers and Shoemaker (1971) hypothesize that the rate of adoption (up to and including the implementation decision) is ". . . faster by the authoritative approach than by the participative approach" (p. 314). However, this hypothesis should not be considered in isolation. As they further emphasize: "Changes brought about by the authoritative approach are more likely to be discontinued than those brought about by the participative approach" (p. 314). Therefore, one major reason many organizations have introduced the participative approach is that it is supposed to increase the rate of successful implementations. The underlying assumption is that when members become more involved in decision making, they will be more eager to implement the changes these decisions involve and thus potentially reduce resistance to change (Coch and French, 1948; Marrow, Bowers, and Seashore, 1967; Watson, 1971). Other reasons for applying the participative approach is that it is supposed to increase the number of new ideas (innovations) proposed (Maier, 1970) and increase the information gathering and processing capabilities of the organization (Duncan, 1973).

It has been pointed out by Wilson (1966) that the extent to which the participative approach facilitates implementation or stimulates proposals of new ideas depends on

. . . the extent to which the decision making group itself becomes a highly valued source of incentives, and the extent to which these group-based incentives are congruent with those offered by the larger organization (p. 212).

This means that the participative approach facilitates innovation only when organizational members feel some benefit or reward for their efforts.

Collective Decisions

In collective decisions the members of the multimember adoption unit usually engage in some type of voting or polling whereby it is determined whether the innovation is to be implemented. Examples of collective decisions are those made in most voluntary organizations and groups and those made on more-or-less controversial issues in communities. Rogers and Shoemaker (1971) have defined the collective decision as one where individuals in a social system adopt or reject by consensus and where all must conform to the system's decision. In discussing decision making in small groups, Schein (1969) notes that decisions made by majority rule are "surprisingly often" not well implemented even by the group that made the decision. He points at two psychological barriers that are likely to lead to implementation problems:

> (1) The minority member often feels that there was an insufficient period of discussion for him to really get his point of view across; hence he feels misunderstood and sometimes resentful.
> (2) The minority member often feels that the voting has created two camps within the group, that these camps are now in win-lose competition, that his camp lost the first round but that it is just a matter of time until it can regroup, pick up some support, and win the next time a vote comes up (p. 56).

Schein (1969, p. 56) suggests rather that decision by consensus is more effective. Here participants believe that the communication processes and group climate have been such that each member feels he has had a fair chance to influence the decision process. There is no formal voting on a decision but rather someone "tests for the 'sense of the meeting,'. . . If there is a clear alternative which most members subscribe to, and if those who oppose it feel they have had their chance to influence, then a consensus exists" (p. 56).

Studying community controversies related to the innovation of fluoridation, Sanders (1961) observed that during the implementation stage the losing side may or may not consider the issue settled. It appears that if the issue is *not* considered settled, two types of activities may occur that are not mutually exclusive: (a) the implementation is delayed because of resistance among individuals or groups whose behavior change is necessary for a successful implementation; (b) the losing side forces the issue to the community forefront again, and the phases of the initiation stage repeat in a second or even a third sequence. Although point (a) perhaps is more common during the implementation stage following an authority decision, point (b) is a frequently occurring activity after a collective decision has been made. Both points concern activities that reduce the rate of successful implementation.

In the remaining part of this book, few explicit references are made to the distinction between authority and collective decisions. Since the 'bias' of this book is in the direction of formal organizations, that is, authority decision, it is briefly indicated below what difference it may make in terms of "stages-variables interaction," when collective rather than authority decisions are made.

Political processes imply formation of special-interest coalitions. In Harvey and Mills' (1970) model of the innovative situation–innovative solution sequence, formation of such coalitions take place mainly during the stage of implementation. This means that the model of these two authors is basically a sequential model of an innovation process in which an authority decision is made. As noted in the first paragraphs of this section, political processes are more intense during the later substages of the initiation stage when collective rather than authority decisions are made (not considering conflict and bargaining in the "dominant coalition," making authority decisions for a larger adoption unit). For collective decisions, therefore, special-interest coalitions (involving resistance to change) are formed during the later substages of the initiation stage. Also authority decisions typically involve downward communication, whereas the collective process employs both horizontal and upward communication after initiation. For instance, Sanders (1961) found that the first sign of opposition to fluoridation in communities usually came after an official proposal had appeared in advance of a town meeting. On the other hand, since information about authority decisions (without participation) is seldom available to the majority of members before implementation has started, coalitions in this case can be formed at a relatively late point in time.

Cooke (1972) has emphasized that collective decision structures are not as common in formal organizations as in communities or voluntary organizations. Collective decision processes in formal organizations are also different in that they must operate in coordination with authority structures. The authority structure influences collective decision procedures because collective innovation decisions are reviewed and legitimated by the formal hierarchy of authority in the organization.

Collective decision-making structures can also facilitate the innovation process in several ways. First, unless the internal feedback mechanisms in the organization are extremely reliable it may be difficult for individuals in the decision hierarchy to be aware of the need for innovations at the lower levels of the organization. A supervisor might not by himself have the relevant information to suggest innovations on the assembly line. The authority decision structure thus does not take advantage of adopting unit members' knowledge as it applies to the innovation decision process. Second, the collective decision process can facilitate the implementation stage of the innovation decision process even if it slows the decision process down, given the involvement of more individuals. The increase of participation in the decision process is likely to lead to more commitment by participants to working through some of the difficulties they might experience during implementation (Morrow et al., 1967). The collective decision process is most applicable and productive when participants feel that (1) the innovation situation they are working on is relevant to their lives; (2) they have the competence to initiate and implement the innovation; (3) they have the authority to carry out the innovation (Cooke, 1972). When all these conditions are not met, some combination of authority and collective decision structures is more appropriate. For example, if individuals are asked to participate in a decision to implement an innovation that they don't feel is relevant to their job, they might feel that their participation is some kind of manipulation by higher level personnel to make them feel important on minor decisions. Their reaction might be one of rejection and withdrawal from assuming any role in the decision process (Sykes, 1962).

RESISTANCE TO INNOVATION

A discussion of only the adoption of innovations leaves an incomplete picture. Many attempts at innovation fail. One important reason, a very reasonable one, is that the advocated innovation is simply not functional enough; that is, it does not do what it purports to do. However, there are many other reasons why innovations fail to be adopted by organizations and why they may not perform adequately once admission to the organization is achieved.

Resistance and Stages of Innovation Process

As a convenient way of looking at the sources and causes of resistance, we shall group them according to the stage of the innovative process in which they are most likely to be operative. It should be pointed out, however, that many resistance factors operate throughout the process of innovation in organizations.

Initiation Stage: Knowledge-Awareness Substage. At this stage there are several inhibitors of innovations entering the organization. Havelock (1970) discusses some of these at length. First there is the *need for stability*. New knowledge or innovations can disrupt the equilibrium and tend therefore to be blocked by various mechanisms. One mechanism is the *coding scheme barrier* whereby innovations expressed in a jargon foreign to corporation members are rejected. Having its own vocabulary makes it difficult for an organization to communicate with external sources of information. Deutsch (1963) has labeled this a "communication differential" between those in and outside the organization. The diffusion of management science techniques has been slowed because of such communication differentials. Interface problems between different units within an organization, for example, between marketing personnel and production personnel, also constitute communication differentials (Young, 1972). Innovations can also be prevented from entering the organization because of its potential *impact on existing social relationships* within the organization (see Stewart, 1957). As Schon (1967, p. 58) notes, "Innovation theatens also the hierarchy of power and prestige on which the corporation's system of control is built, for its political structure is tied to an established technology." Related to this is the fear that outsiders represent a *personal threat*. It has been observed in several instances that objections, especially among middle management, to hiring consultants are based on a perceived threat to the role and status position occupied by individuals voicing objections. This fear may be rooted in such thoughts that the consultant will be critical of the objectors' role performance or may suggest that their role specifications be altered. Technological innovation can be threatening at all levels of the corporation, particularly to top management for whom the cumulative effects of innovation may be overwhelming. "If the president came up through the business and draws his confidence from his intimate knowledge of the details of the present operation, technological innovation may throw him onto completely unfamiliar ground. He understood the old business; he does not understand the new one. How can he manage if he does not understand the business he is in?" (Schon, 1967, p. 68).

Havelock (1970) suggests that *local pride* may also be an obstacle. The idea that the organization is unique or special in some positive way leads to the belief that alterations in the organization would dissipate this uniqueness. Thus a deaf ear is turned to new knowledge, which may indicate that change is necessary. This has been demonstrated in studies of scientists in organizations (Allen, cited by Havelock, 1970) and in a study of administrators in business firms (President's Conference, cited by Havelock).

Another barrier to the flow of new knowledge to the organization is a status discrepancy between the potential recipient and potential donors (Rice, 1963). The higher the status of the potential donor organization relative to the recipient organization, the less likely information will flow between them (Czepiel, 1972). The rationale behind this is that seeking information is an admission of inferiority.

In addition there must also be a *felt need* for new information or knowledge along with the *economic ability* to utilize or to act upon the new knowledge. If either of these is missing, new knowledge is unlikely to be admitted into the organization (Czepiel, 1972). Pellegrin (1966), speaking in an educational context, notes that barriers to the flow of new knowledge to an organization may stem from weaknesses in channels of communication and weaknesses in the procedure for disseminating new educational ideas.

Attitude Formation and Decision Substages. Once new information or knowledge has entered the organization, a number of factors may become operative that result in rejection of the innovation. As Havelock (1970, pp. 6–22) notes, "Internally the organization can be seen as a complex system of filters; each subsystem and each member has some power to block the flow of information, to screen it, censor it, and distort it." This is related to what Watson (1973) calls systemic coherence: it is difficult to change one part of a system without affecting other parts of the system. Watson notes the example of a technological change that had to be abandoned because it increased the productivity of piece workers to the point where they started earning more money than their supervisors. There are many structural factors in organizations that are sources of resistance. Stratification is another problem. The more stratified the power structure in an organization, the harder it is to engender change *from the bottom up* (Watson, 1973; Rogers, 1973). Hage and Aiken (1970, p. 31) note a related point that the higher the centralization the lower the rate of organizational innovation.

The *division of labor* is another structural factor. The division of labor may create interunit competition; for example, groups sharing common tasks may feel that they are in competition with one another for scarce resources in the firm. Different norms and even goals may develop within the different categories, thereby producing conflict and a lessening of cooperation. This in turn makes decisions difficult to reach. Also if an innovation is first initiated or proposed by one group, competing groups tend to discourage its further development within the organization. As Schein (1970, p. 99) notes: "The fundamental problem of intergroup competition is the conflict of goals and the breakdown of interaction and communication between groups; . . ." For all practical purposes the different subunits are as distinct as different organizations, and the various factors affecting the flow of innovations between organizations or from the external environment to the organization become operative for each submit. Schein (1970, p. 88) further notes with regard to problems inherent in forming a new interdepartmental committee—which itself may be an innovation in some situations—to consider the adoption of an innovation that "Each person is likely to be so concerned about the group he came from, wishing to uphold its interests as its representative, that it becomes difficult for the members to become identified with the new committee." (p. 88) The dysfunctional consequence of this is that the lack of commitment to the committee engenders a lack of commitment or support to the particular innovation the specially constituted committee was formed to consider.

Roles can be inhibiting or facilitative. Havelock (1970) appears to feel that roles function primarily to maintain the status quo: "Most role expectations are designed to stabilize and routinize human performance. They encourage conformity . . . The more sharply defined and the more limited the role, the less room there will be for receiving and sending messages which are 'new' and hence different from what is expected" (pp. 6–22). Hage and Aiken (1970) also make this observation. They claim that formalization, the degree of codification of jobs in an organization, is inversely related to the rate of innovation.

Hierarchical and status differentials are additional sources of resistance to change operating during the attitude formation and decision process stages. Fear of depreciating one's own status within the organization can cause considerable resistance; when such fears are widespread within firms the organization can be immobilized with regard to change (Burns and Stalker, 1961). This has been noted in several organizational contexts ranging from hospitals to community governments. It has been postulated that "the more hierarchical the structure of an organization the less the possibility of change" (Griffiths, 1964, p. 434). *Physical separation* is con-

ducive to noninnovative decision making, but physical separation is often a symptom or manifestation of hierarchical and
status differences.

Reward patterns may also tend to produce conservative
rather than innovative decision making. Typically individuals
are rewarded for stable, reliable behavior, a type of behavior
not conducive to being a product champion (Rothe, 1960;
Schon, 1967). When innovative behavior is rewarded by the
organization, the behavior is more likely to have involved
modest innovativeness rather than radical innovativeness.

Implementation Stage: Initial Implementation Substage.
Effective resistance can readily occur at the implementation
stage. We quote extensively from Graziano (1969, p. 12) on
this point.

> Thus when innovation intrudes, the structure responds with
> various strategies to deal with the threat; it might incorporate the
> new event and alter it to fit the preexisting structure so that, in ef-
> fect, nothing is really changed. It might deal with it also by active re-
> jection, calling upon all of its resources to 'starve out' the innovator by
> insuring a lack of support.
> The most subtle defense, however, is to ostensibly accept and
> encourage the innovator, to publicly proclaim support of innovative
> goals, and while doing that to build in various controlling safeguards,
> such as special committees, thereby insuring that the work is always
> accomplished through power structure channels and thus effecting no
> real change. This tactic achieves the nullification of the innovator
> while at the same time giving the power structure the public sem-
> blance of progressiveness. The power structure can become so in-
> volved in this pose that the lower-line personnel come to honestly
> believe that they are working for the stated ideals such as humanitar-
> ianism, science, and progress, while in reality they labor to maintain
> the political power of the status quo.
> Hence while the power structure continues to proclaim innova-
> tion, it expends great energy to insure, through its defensive maneu-
> vers, the maintenance of its status quo. Innovation is thus allowed,
> and even encouraged, as long as it remains on the level of conceptual
> abstractions, and provided that it does not, in reality, change any-
> thing!

Resistance can be expected at the implementation stage for several reasons. First, disequilibrium is greatest at this stage and conflict more severe as the innovation becomes an organizational reality. Disequilibrium is likely because all contingencies cannot be anticipated and planned for. Conflict may be especially acute if the innovation involves establishing new job positions. Those in the new positions seek to acquire as many resources as possible to ensure the success of the innovation. Typically, these resources are obtained at the expense of some other part of the organization, thereby creating strain or outright conflict between those who lose the scarce resources and those who gain them.

Passive resistance is another form of rejection by individuals further down the line. This involves simply not following through on directives issued by top management or not utilizing the innovation to its fullest capacity or in proper ways. For example, in a number of school systems the school principals ordered educational simulation games for use in the classroom. For various reasons the games were frequently left on the shelf or used halfheartedly and thus somewhat ineffectively. This failure to use the simulation games in their most effective way provided a basis in some schools for the decision by the school principal not to pursue the concept of academic gaming further. The teachers simply said, "we tried it but it didn't work." The school principal had no way of knowing how fair a test these innovations had in the classroom. Had the teachers in school systems been involved in the decision process, the innovation may have met with greater success.

Argyris (1970) indicates several factors producing resistance when an innovation is implemented on a unilateral basis by top management. Resistance increases during the implementation of an innovation because of the ". . . (b) mistrust and condemnation of the subordinates implied by the new program, (c) the inhibition of the questions and fears, the subordinates wished to express *before* they were 'sold', (d) the feelings of being manipulated by the fact that the changes were kept a secret . . ." (p. 72).

Thus failure of key personnel to cooperate is an important source of resistance during the implementation stage. Hage and Aiken (1970) also make this observation in a case description of the adoption of therapeutic patient care in a mental hospital:

> The chief of staff and administration were wholeheartedly in favor of this innovation, but the psychiatrists, nurses, attendants, and some others had to alter their behavior toward the patient if the program was to be a success. In other words job descriptions of many jobs had to be altered. Since these specialists were most intimately involved with the innovation, they were in a position to sabotage the new program, subtly if they so desired (p. 102).

Thus the implementation stage is a stage of considerable potential conflict and perhaps the stage during which disequilibrium is greatest. The innovation becomes a reality, and latent animosities, feelings of loss of power, and so on are apt to become manifest. Also at this stage short-run effects of unforeseen and unintended negative consequences of innovations become known.

Continued-Sustained Implementation Substage. Once an innovation has become implemented, it may subsequently be rejected or discontinued. There is very little in the published literature concerning the discontinuance of innovations in organizations or even of innovations intended solely for use by individuals. The innovation may fail to perform adequately even when all factors are supportive and thus be discontinued on a performance basis only. Continued conflict among components of the organization over the innovation may be disruptive to the point where the value of the innovation falls below the social conflicts it engenders. Also, as time goes by after the initial implementation period there is increased opportunity for the long-range ill effects of the innovation to become evident. As these events become obvious and accumulate, resistance may become stronger and more widespread.

An innovation may be discontinued because of personnel changes. New school principals, hospital administrators, product development managers have been known to disregard recent changes soon after they establish themselves in their new positions. Several reasons for this have been given, the most noteworthy perhaps is that it is a way to make their presence felt and to prevent the development of interest groups and power centers forming around these recent changes. The commitment of personnel to recent changes makes it more difficult to develop commitment for changes the new manager may advocate.

Coe and Barnhill (1967) present some interesting insights into the failure of an implemented innovation that had been widely supported at the time of its implementation. They suggest two possible causes for resistance leading to the failure of the innovation and the reversion to *status quo ante*. The innovation in this case was a new medications system having its primary impact on nursing personnel. The first explanation is the halo effect. The initial strong positive response among the nursing staff to the innovation as a whole was attributed to the strong appeal of one particular aspect of the innovation. This one attractive feature was generalized to other aspects of the medication system when the innovation was first implemented. However, as increasing experience was gained with the medication system the negative features began to assert themselves. In fact this suggests the possibility of a negative halo or devil's horns effect.

A second explanation of why the innovation met with resistance during the continuance stage concerns the "disruption of the social organization of the nursing unit and a loss of authority by the head nurse." (Coe and Barnhill, 1967, p. 155). In addition to introducing new procedures, the new system made alterations in roles and statuses within the nursing unit. The head nurse under the new system lost a degree of control and authority over her subordinates and hence experienced an associated loss of flexibility in rewarding and punishing other nurses.

Individual Resistance Processes

Organizational decision making is in large measure a function of individual decision making, and for this reason it is useful to look at resistance in the individual decision-making process under conditions of innovation. The resistance factors noted are drawn primarily from Watson (1973). Additional treatments of psychological resistance to change can be found in Foster (1962), Gibb (1961), and Coch and French (1948). The resistance forces are presented at the stage in which they are most likely to be operative (see Figure 2-4); it must be stressed, however, that separate psychological forces can be operative at more than one stage. Some elaboration of each stage is presented to facilitate the understanding of how each resistance force operates.

Perception. The internal process begins with perception. Both the innovation and the need must be perceived by the individual for eventual adoption to occur. Time sequence at this stage would not appear to be significant, for either the individual's need or the innovation could be the initial perception without affecting the ultimate outcome.

Often, it seems, investigators impose their perceptions on others to achieve "proper" classification, when the important perceptions are those of the individual being studied. Different research outcomes can be expected depending on whose view is being employed. An outstanding example of this problem is given by Bennett (1969) in classifying newcomers in a dynamic society. They may be "precocious" when they

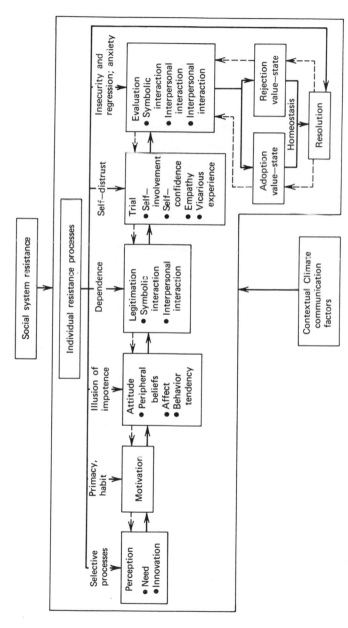

Figure 2-4. A resistance-adoption model.

adopt a behavior upon their early exposure to it in the society, despite the fact that the product had already achieved wide acceptance in the society. The precocious individual who adopts almost immediately because of the newness of the product to him is most likely an innovator, but may be classified as a laggard by the investigator who is unaware of the situation. Thus the investigator's perception of the situation may have an important, but perhaps unfortunate, impact on the research findings.

It is likely that perceptions of an innovation by the individual adopter change as he moves through the various stages of adoption. What is seen as new or different in the early stages may eventually be thought of as commonplace in the later stages, and vice versa. Changes in perception such as these would have important effects on individual behavior. Thus perception should be traced through the entire process for possible changes. Do innovators change their perceptions more rapidly than others? Or do they adopt because of the newness involved, whereas others require more familiarity with the product? Conceivably, too, early adopters may be such because they see the item as familiar (Zaltman and Dubois, 1971).

The obvious factors affecting the individual at this stage are the selective processes, both selective perception and selective retention. More than just a result of currently held attitudes, these processes may originate as a result of the cultural (Rogers and Shoemaker, 1971), social, or communicative climate.

Motivation. A necessary step in overcoming natural resistance to change is motivation. Behaviors that are comfortable (habit) are normally resistant to change, as are those that represent the first successful attempt at solving a given problem (primacy). Individual perceptions of the existing need and the innovation must provide the impetus for further action, thus overcoming these and other possible personality-based resistances.

Attitude. The next stage of the process is attitude. Kelman and Warrick (1973, p. 25) observe that "the very functioning attitudes—the way they affect the person's exposure to new information, his perception and memory, and his action toward the attitude object—tends to build and maintain support for the attitude and thus lead to resistance to change."

The attitude stage contains three components suggested by numerous sources: cognitive, affective, and behavioral (Summers, 1970). As the individual moves through this stage, he develops beliefs about the innovation based on information he develops in his social interactions, in reading advertisements, in reviewing reports on the product published in various consumer magazines, and so on. Beliefs of this type have been classified as peripheral beliefs. They are based on information supplied by authorities who are viewed by the consumer as being trustworthy (Rokeach, 1968). Recent work by Jacoby is enlightening for authority-based beliefs and action tendencies (Jacoby 1971a and b). Such beliefs are subject to change if the authorities from which they are derived change position, or they may be replaced if more basic beliefs contradict the peripheral beliefs.

The affective component at this stage probably is not strong. It may be limited to liking or disliking the product or idea. The strength or intensity of this emotional component supplies the impetus for the behavior that follows. Greater intensity may mean a more rapid progression through the remaining stages of the process. Research on this component could reveal the actions of such factors as acceptance or repression of emotion in the behavior of innovators and laggards, as well as the effects of the strength of this emotional component on rapidity of adoption or rejection.

An important type of resistance at this stage is the individual's illusion of his own impotence. It seems quite likely that this could reduce the affect felt by the individual, with a lowered behavioral tendency as a result. Such an outcome at this stage might cause the process to remain incomplete (Zaltman and Stiff, 1973).

Legitimation. The legitimation state is when the individual seeks reinforcement for the action he is contemplating. The appropriateness of the action is of prime importance. This may be determined by the individual by observing performance of the behavior by others in his group or by seeking affirmation from his peers, relatives, and so on. Interactions seem to be an important criterion for recognizing occurrence of the legitimation stage. Lack of interaction, then, is a source of resistance. Although their study was based on another model, the work of Pareek and Singh (1969) lends support to this position. Their study showed increasing interactions that peaked just prior to the trial stage.

The resistance process most likely to occur here is dependence. The fact that the individual looks to others for support is a reflection of an earlier stage of life when parents supplied emotional support to the child. When people receive such support from others, they tend to adopt the outlook of those others, thus maintaining a conservative position toward change and perpetuating the status quo.

Trial. The trial stage is that which is commonly accepted. The individual puts the innovation to a personal test prior to complete acceptance. Occasionally, however, the nature of the innovation (Lin and Zaltman, 1973) or the situation may make personal testing impossible, and the individual may "try" the innovation through vicarious experience (Bandura, 1969), with results similar to those of personal testing. The individual who lacks confidence in his own ability may have unsatisfactory experiences here.

Evaluation. Evaluation is a necessary formal step between the trial and adoption stages. Following trial, the individual reviews the pros and cons of continued or increased use. The existence of this stage was uncovered in the Pareek and Singh study, their evidence being a high level of interaction following the trial stage in which interaction was almost nonexistent. Although it is quite likely that informal or very brief evaluation follows each stage in the adoption process to review the situation to that point, a formal evaluation is probably necessary before a formal commitment is made. Therefore, evaluation should precede adoption in the model.

Insecurity and regression may cause the individual to discount the effects of the trial stage, as life before the introduction of complexity may seem more attractive. Previous behavior patterns resulted in a modicum of success in coping with life, and those are favorably recalled. Anxiety may also evoke this response because of the potential threat involved in adopting a new behavior.

Adoption or Rejection. The stage of adoption represents a level of commitment by the individual with repeated or continued usage. This is also a stage with cognitive, affective, and behavioral components. There is quite a difference between this stage and the attitude stage, however. The cognitive component at the adoption stage contains beliefs based on personal experience from the trial stage. These beliefs are more basic and strongly held than the beliefs of the attitude stage (Rokeach, 1968). They may supplement or supplant the beliefs that are less basic.

The emotional component is also likely to be stronger than in the attitude stage. It is only logical that it takes a greater incentive to commit oneself to a continuous behavior pattern of use than merely to continue consideration of such use.

The depth of commitment and the belief change move

this stage toward what might be termed a value state. This approaches greater centrality in psychological position than does an attitude and becomes a basis against which other possible states are measured. The stronger the adoption commitment that is made, the more central will be the value state achieved. An innovation that would enable the individual to achieve some deeply held goal would indeed be difficult to replace.

The alternative to adoption, at this point, is rejection. Unsatisfactory outcomes in the process prior to this stage may result in the achieved value stage being negative. The components of rejection are the same as those of adoption and achieve similar intensity.

Resolution. The final stage is that of resolution (Campbell, 1966). This concept includes dissonance reduction, but it is more inclusive. Dissonance is not the inevitable result of adoption. Some innovations are adopted without regret, even enthusiastically. Dissonance may result when one is forced to choose between two or more attractive alternatives, but some innovations may be far superior to anything previously known or may be the only known alternative available to solve a problem. Thus the concept of dissonance may be somewhat overly restrictive or misleading. The broader perspective suggested by resolution could lead to fruitful investigative results. The idea of perpetuating the achieved state is represented here by the resistance process of homeostasis.

Another framework for viewing the rejection of innovations is shown in Table 2-4. This particular table was developed by Eichholtz and Rogers in reference to individuals located in educational organizations. However, it appears to have considerable generalizability to other organizational contexts. Guidelines for reducing resistance to change have been presented by Watson (1973) and are shown in Figure 2-5. However, and this is an important point, resistance

Table 2-4. A Framework for the Identification of Forms of Rejection

Form of Rejection	Cause of Rejection	State of Subject	Anticipated Response
Ignorance	Lack of dissemination	Uninformed	"The information is not easily available."
Suspended Judgment	Data not *logically* compelling	Doubtful	"I want to wait and see how good it is before I try."
Situational	Data not *materially* compelling	1. Comparing	"Other things are equally as good."
		2. Defensive	"The school regulations will not permit it."
		3. Deprived	"It costs too much to use in time and/or money."
Personal	Data not *psychologically* compelling	1. Anxious	"I don't know if I can operate equipment
		2. Guilty	"I know I should use them, but I don't have time."
		3. Alienated	"These gadgets will never replace a teacher."
Experimental	Present or past trials	Convinced	"I tried them once and they aren't any good."

(From Eicholtz and Rogers, 1964)

Observations on sources of resistance within persons and within institutions can be summarized in some concise principles. These are not absolute laws but are based on generalizations that are usually true and likely to be pertinent. The recommendations are here reorganized to answer three questions: Who brings the change? What kind of change succeeds? How is it best done—by what procedures and in what climate?

A. *Who brings the change?*
   1. Resistance will be less if persons involved, teachers, board members, and community leaders, feel that the project is their own—not one devised and operated by outsiders.
   2. Resistance will be less if the project clearly has wholehearted support from top officials of the system.

B. *What kind of change?*
   3. Resistance will be less if participants see the change as reducing rather than increasing their present burdens.
   4. Resistance will be less if the project accords with values and ideals that have long been acknowledged by participants.
   5. Resistance will be less if the program offers the kind of *new* experience that interests participants.
   6. Resistance will be less if participants feel that their autonomy and their security are not threatened.

C. *Procedures in instituting change*
   7. Resistance will be less if participants have joined in diagnostic

Figure 2-5.   Reducing resistance: a summary (From Watson, 1973)

may be desirable. As Klein (1967) and others (Stiles and Robinson, 1973; Warwick and Kelman, 1973) point out, resistance can be useful. Not all change is healthy; "new" should not automatically be equated with "good." Klein (1967, p. 30) puts forth a major thesis that "a necessary prerequisite of successful change involves the mobilization of forces against it." Resistance may highlight problems in the organization and bring forth or require more detailed and careful reasoning by the proponents of the innovation. Indirectly, the threat of resistance causes the advocates of change to plan

efforts leading them to agree on the basic problem and to feel
its importance.

8. Resistance will be less if the project is adopted by consensual
group decision.

9. Resistance will be reduced if proponents are able to empa-
thize with opponents, to recognize valid objections, and to take
steps to relieve unnecessary fears.

10. Resistance will be reduced if it is recognized that innovations
are likely to be misunderstood and misinterpreted, and if provision is made for feedback of perceptions of the project and
for further clarification as needed.

11. Resistance will be reduced if participants experience acceptance, support trust, and confidence in their relations with
one another.

12. Resistance will be reduced if the project is kept open to revi-
sion and reconsideration if experience indicates that changes
would be desirable.

D. *Climate for change*

13. Readiness for change gradually becomes a characteristic of
certain individuals, groups, organizations, and civilizations.
They no longer look nostalgically at a golden age in the past
but anticipate their utopia in days to come. The spontaneity
of youth is cherished and innovations are protected until they
have had a chance to establish their worth. The ideal is more
and more seen as possible.

Figure 2-5.   continued

ahead and anticipate possible negative consequences of the innovation.

SUMMARY

This chapter has focused on innovation as an acceptance or
decision-making process. Although alternative decision-making processes for collectivities are reviewed, one particular
process is featured. This model involves two basic steps or

stages. First is the initiation stage which involves the following substages: knowledge awareness, formation of attitudes,
and decision. The second stage is the implementation stage,
which involves two substages: initial implementation and
continued-sustained implementation. Control of the innovation process, including the notion of feedback, is also discussed, as are two basic classes of innovative decisions. The
phenomenon of resistance is analyzed at two levels. First, resistance is considered within the framework of the two stage
models mentioned, which is relevant for organizations per se.
Next, resistance is considered within the framework of the
individual's adoption process. The various sources of resistance discussed are only suggestive of the many factors acting
as constraints on innovation adoption in organizations.
Clearly one area of research in organization behavior concerns the interrelatedness of attributes of innovations and the
several sources of resistance both at the macro or organizational level and at the micro or individual level.

NOTES

1. This discussion of decision making is intended as a brief over-
    view. For more detailed discussions, see March and Simon (1958),
    Taylor (1965), and Shull et al. (1970).
2. These authority innovative decisions are discussed in a later sec-
    tion of this chapter.
3. For a more complete discussion of various change strategies, the
    context in which they are most appropriate, and general criteria
    for selecting strategies, see Gerald Zaltman and Robert Duncan,
    Strategies of Planned Change Forthcoming, Wiley-Interscience.
4. These organizational characteristics are discussed in detail in
    Chapter 3.

3 Characteristics of Organizations Affecting Innovation

INTRODUCTION

In the previous two chapters, the nature and processes of innovation have been discussed—the various types of innovations and their attributes in (Chapter 1) and the phases of the innovation process in (Chapter 2). In this chapter we (1) discuss organizational environments; (2) discuss the bureaucratic organization as it relates to innovation; and (3) present a modified view of organization structure emphasizing the characteristics of organizations as they affect the process of innovation.

Organization Defined

The concept of organization has been defined in a variety of ways (see Parsons, 1956; Katz and Kahn, 1966; Caplow, 1964). In this analysis an organization is defined *as a social system created for attaining some specific goals through the collective efforts of its members. Its most salient characteristic is its structure that specifies its operation.* In a later section of this chapter, we discuss organizational structure in some detail.

The general characteristics of social systems have been noted by various authors (Miller, 1965; Bertalanffy, 1968), and these are briefly mentioned as they apply to organizations. As a system there is an *importation of energy* from the external environment into the organization. Here is where the organization gets resources from the environment in terms of people, raw materials, capital, and so forth. Once these inputs are available to the organization, the organization creates something at this *through-put stage*. It is at this point that the organization transforms the raw materials from the environment into some product or service. It is during this through-put stage that innovations move from the initiation stage into the implementation stage. Finally, the organization's product or service that has been developed during the through-put cycle is exported and exchanged as *output* with the environment. The output is then exchanged in the external environment for new inputs, and the cycle starts anew. The organization's survival, then, depends on its ability to favorably exchange its outputs over time with the environment to get continued inputs. For example, during the late 1960s and early 1970s graduate schools in United States universities faced a decline in the demand for their output of new PhD's. This decline in demand for graduate schools' output resulted in problems of obtaining new inputs. Because the demand for new PhD's had declined, there were fewer funds available from both federal and private sources to support existing as well as new educational programs. Thus universities are now rethinking degree programs to develop outputs that are more favorably received by the larger environment.

In emphasizing the importance of this exchange between the organization and its environment, some organizational theorists have suggested that a new view of organizational effectiveness be considered. Yuchtman and Seashore (1967) argue that the goal approach to assessing effectiveness should be avoided "first, because goals as ideal states do not offer the possibility of realistic assessment; second, goals as cultural entities arise outside of the organization as a social system and cannot arbitrarily be attributed as properties of the organization itself" (p. 893). The authors also indicate that the functional approach is unacceptable in assessing effectiveness, because some frame of reference for comparison must be used in evaluating the organization. The effectiveness of the organization can be judged in relation to its own welfare or according to how successful the organization is in contributing to the success of some other system (Yuchtman and Seashore, 1967, p. 895). The problem then is always what frame of reference to use in making the evaluation.

Yuchtman and Seashore suggest a systems resource ap-

Table 3-1. Performance Factors Indicating Organizations' Ability to Exploit Environment for Scarce Resources

Factor	Assigned Name	Number Assigned Variable	Indicator Variables
I	Business volume *	Ia	Number of policies in force (year's end)
		Ib	New insurance sold (dollar volume)
		Ic	Renewal premiums collected (dollars)
		Id	Number of lives insured (year's end)
		Ie	Agency manpower (number of agents)
II	Production cost	IIa	Production cost per new policy
		IIb	Production cost per $1000 of insurance
		IIc	Production cost per $100 of premium
III	New member productivity	IIIa	Average productivity per new agent
		IIIb	Ratio of new agent versus old agent productivity (new agent less than 5 years of service)
IV	Youthfulness of members	IVa	Ratio of younger (under 35) to total membership
		IVb	Ratio of productivity of younger members to total members of agency

Table 3-1. (continued)

Factor	Assigned Name	Number Assigned Variable	Indicator Variables
V	Business mix †	Va	Average premium per $1000
		Vb	Percentage of new policies with quarterly payments
		Vc	Percentage of business in employee trust
VI	Manpower growth	VIa	Net change in manpower during year
		VIb	Ratio of net change to initial manpower
VII	Management emphasis	VIIa	Manager's personal commissions
VIII	Maintenance cost ‡	VIIIa	Maintenance cost per collection
		VIIIb	Maintenance cost per $100 premium collected
IX	Member productivity	IXa	Average new business volume per agent
X	Market penetration	Xa	Insurance in force per capita
		Xb	Number of lives covered per 1000 insurables

(From Seashore and Yuchtman 1967:383)
* Including both accumulated volume and current increment in volume.
† Many low-value transactions vs. fewer high value transactions.
‡ Refers to maintenance of accounts, not of physical facilities.

proach to organizational effectiveness. Effectiveness is defined in terms of the organization's ". . . bargaining position, as reflected in the ability of the organization, in either absolute or relative terms, to exploit its environment in the acquisition of scarce and valued resources" (Yuchtman and Seashore, 1967, p. 898). In a factor analysis of 76 performance indicators in 75 insurance sales agencies over an 11-year period, Seashore and Yuchtman (1967) found 10 factors that described most of the variance. In reviewing these factors, presented in Table 3-1, Seashore and Yuchtman (1967, p. 392) concluded that they represent an organization's ability to exploit its environment for scarce resources.

ORGANIZATIONAL ENVIRONMENTS

From the foregoing discussion it is apparent that the organization as conceptualized here is not a closed system. Rather, the organization is viewed as an open system in continued interaction with its environment. Given the importance of the interaction between the organization and its environment, it is necessary to discuss more fully organizational environments as they affect the innovation process.

The environment of a multimember adoption unit is important in two different ways. First, changes in the environment create a *situation* of stress or pressure to which the adoption unit must respond if it is to remain in a relationship of "dynamic equilibrium" with the environment. Thus an adoption unit is more likely to innovate when its relevant environment is rapidly changing than when it is steady. In this sense, environment includes such factors as technological changes, market conditions, and clientle needs and demands (See Burns and Stalker, 1961). Second, if the response to the situation is an innovative *solution*, environmental norms may or may not favor the changes this solution implies. This means that during the implementation stage not only internal but also external resistance to change may occur, and both internal and external special-interest coalitions may be formed. It might be hypothesized that successful implementation is more likely when the larger social environment to which the adoption unit belongs has norms that favor change (See Rogers, 1962).

For example, some school systems have attempted to expand their curriculum by introducing sex education programs. Often these program innovations are not successful because citizen groups in the larger community band together to resist the innovation as an encroachment of the parent's right to control the sex education of his child. Thus the norms of the external environment do not support the innovation of the organization.

Mohr (1969) also provides a brief analysis of the relationship between innovative *solutions* and environmental norms. Studying differences in innovation among local health departments, Mohr takes a closer look at the community in which a department is situated, trying to identify the degree to which the former is prepared to accept or resist departures from established practices (innovations). Applying education and occupation as measures of social class levels in the community, he finds that only occupation is related strongly enough to innovation to retain at least some independent explanatory power (in terms of partial correlation) (p. 118). But the occupation level (extent of white-collar employment) does not provide a great deal of additional explanatory power once the size of community is considered. Nevertheless, Mohr says:

We will keep in mind . . . that if extent of innovation seems to be determined by community size, the reason may be partly in a relationship between size and social class characteristics. At some level of probability, for example, the larger the health jurisdiction, the greater the percent white collar, and therefore the greater the readiness to accept innovations in public programs (p. 119).

When studying the impact of environmental changes upon multimember adoption units, it is of crucial importance to note the following statement by Wilson (1966). "Environmental changes that to the outside observer 'objectively' seem to 'require' innovation by the organization (adoption unit), are likely to lead to such innovation only insofar as these changes alter the preferences of members for incentives (by changing present or prospective costs of benefits of participation in the organization)" (p. 210). In terms of the process model in Chapter 2 this citation is especially important for evaluation of, and choice among, alternatives. Outside observers who claim that an organization has failed to innovate or adapt to environmental pressures often make their judgement in terms of the adoption unit's publicly stated goals and what is supposed to be necessary in order to attain those goals. But, as Wilson points out, ". . . whether a failure to attain a goal will lead to innovation depends on whether members regard attainment of (or work toward) that goal as a reward of participation" (Wilson, 1966, p. 210). For instance, if a business firm has the official goal of profit maximization, whereas rewards for management are mainly produced by a favorable sales position, an innovative alternative may not be chosen for implementation unless the sales position is expected to become improved. Thus a distinction between individual incentives in terms of rewards and organizational goals seems to be one important factor in explaining failure to innovate or adapt to environmental changes.

Utterback's (1971a) work has emphasized the importance of the organization's environment in the innovation process by indicating that the primary limitations on an organization's effectiveness in innovation are neither the costs nor the technical knowledge required. Rather, the primary limitations ". . . appear to be its ability and perhaps aggressiveness in recognizing needs and demands in its external environment" (p. 81).

There has been a great deal of discussion in organizational theory emphasizing that organizations need to adapt to and influence their environment to remain viable social systems (Parsons, 1956). Organizations need to learn to influence their environment and have some degree of control over it if they are to be effective over time. Thompson (1967, p. 32) has also pointed out that organizations seek to minimize their dependence on various elements in their environment. For example, a manufacturing organization would try to avoid being dependent on a single supplier for a particular component. The organization would seek to maintain alternative suppliers of the component or perhaps would consider producing the component themselves.

Organizational Environment Defined (1)

One of the shortcomings of much of the theoretical and empirical research on organizational environments has been the failure to clearly conceptualize the environment or the elements comprising it (Lawrence and Lorsch, 1967a; Emery and Trist, 1965). Pugh et al. (1968) have studied organizational contexts such as origin and history, ownership control, size, and location, that are the settings within which organizational structure is developed. However, as they have specified, this is not a model of an organization in an environment. Lawrence and Lorsch (1967a), for example, have studied how organizations segment their environment into related sectors, but they do not clearly conceptualize the environment or its makeup. They have also conceptualized the environment as a total entity but have looked only at the environment from the organization outward (p. 4). Dills' (1958) concept of the task environment again focused only on those parts of the organization's *external* environment (customers, suppliers of labor, capital, materials, competitors for both resources and markets, and regulatory groups) that are relevant or potentially relevant to the organization's goal setting and goal attainment.

Organizational environment is, then, defined as the totality of physical and social factors that are taken *directly into consideration* in the decision-making behavior of individuals in the organization. If the environment is defined in this way, there clearly are factors *within* the boundaries of the organizational activities that must be considered as part of the environment. Therefore, a differentiation is made between the system's internal and external environment.

The *internal environment* consists of those relevant physical and social factors *within* the boundaries of the organization or specific decision unit that are taken directly into consideration in the decision-making behavior of individuals in that system. For example, the internal environment for an industrial organization would consist of the various departments and personnel making up that organization.

The *external environment* consists of those relevant physical and social factors *outside* the boundaries of the organization or specific decision unit that are taken directly into consideration in the decision-making behavior of individuals in that system. For example, the external environment of the above industrial organization would consist of suppliers, customers, regulatory groups, and so forth.

Components of the Environment as They Affect Innovation

A more detailed outline of environmental components is presented in Table 3-2. The list of environmental components presented may be particularly relevant to industrial organizations and may vary for other types of organizations. However, this goes beyond the existing research (Dill, 1958;

Table 3-2. Factors and Components Comprising the Organization's Internal and External Environment

Internal Environment	External Environment
Organizational personnel component A. Educational and technological background and skills B. Previous technological and managerial skill C. Individual member's involvement and commitment to attaining system's goals D. Interpersonal behavior styles E. Availability of manpower for utilization within the system Organizational functional and staff units component A. Technological characteristics of organizational units B. Interdependence of organizational units in carrying out their objectives C. Intraunit conflict among organizational functional and staff units D. Interunit conflict among organizational functional and staff units Organizational level component A. Organizational objectives and goals B. Integrative process integrating individuals and groups into contributing maximally to attaining organizational goals C. Nature of the organization's product service	Customer component A. Distributors of product or service B. Actual users of product or service Suppliers component A. New materials suppliers B. Equipment suppliers C. Product parts suppliers D. Labor supply Competitor component A. Competitors for suppliers B. Competitors for customers Socio-political component A. Government regulatory control over the industry B. Public political attitude towards industry and its particular product C. Relationship with trade unions with jurisdiction in the organization Technological component A. Meeting new technological requirements of own industry and related industries in production of product or service B. Improving and developing new products by implementing new technological advances in the industry

(From Duncan 1972a, p. 315)

115

Lawrence and Lorsch, 1967a; Emery and Trist, 1965) by more clearly conceptualizing the environment and factors comprising it. A list such as this might be developed for a decision unit to act as a guide for gathering information in decision making.

It should be emphasized that no decision maker would be expected to identify all these components as part of the organization's internal or external environment for a specific decision situation. Rather, the makeup of the environment is expected to change over time. For example, a programming and planning decision unit's environment in developing one type of product might focus on customer demand and the marketing and production departments. In planning and developing programs for a different type of product, the relevant environment to be considered in decision making may have changed to include, in addition to the marketing and production departments, a different group of customers, and possibly government regulatory agencies with jurisdiction over this type of product. This specification of what part of the environment to focus on in decision making identifies the domain problem where decision unit members must identify what aspects of the environment are to be of concern in decision making. (McWhinney, 1968, p. 272)

The domain problem is most crucial in the innovation process because defining the domain indicates what part of the environment the organization must consider relevant in its decision making. The question, becomes, what is the important domain in the innovation process?

In studying how organizations scan their environment in decision making, Aguilar (1967) has investigated the relative importance of different types of information from the environment. Aguilar's findings are presented in Table 3-3. They indicate that the most important sources of information for the organization is the market. In fact, the market accounted for 58% of all responses, which is more than 3 times the

Table 3-3.   Relative Importance of Areas of External Information Overall Data, All Managers (Percent of Responses)

Area of External Information	Percent of Total Responses	Information Category	Percent of Total Responses
Market tidings	58	Market potential	30
		Structural change	10
		Competitors and industry	4
		Pricing	4
		Sales negotiations	6
		Customers	4
Technical tidings	18*	New products, etc.	14
		Product problems	2
		Costs	1
		Licensing and patents	3
Broad issues	8	General conditions	4
		Government actions, etc.	4
Acquisition leads	7	Leads for mergers, etc.	7
Other tidings	9	Suppliers, etc.	5
		Resources available	2
		Miscellaneous	2
Total percent	100		102*
Total number of responses	190		190

(From Aguilar 1967, p. 43)
* Error due to rounding.

amount of information coming from the technical area. This dominance of market information leads Aguilar to conclude that ". . . companies tend to react to current conditions rather than to innovate" (p. 54). These results thus indicate that the most important domain for the organization is the market.

The importance of this external information and needs is also supported by the research on idea generation by Baker et al. (1967). This research indicates that there are two kinds of information required at the *idea generation stage* in innovation. First, there has to be some knowledge of a need that is relevant to the organization. Second, there must be some knowledge of a means or technique for satisfying the need (p. 156). The results of their research on 300 ideas created in a divisional laboratory of a large company indicated several things. Need events stimulated 75% of the ideas, whereas 25% of the ideas were stimulated by a knowledge of a means, which was then followed by knowledge of some need (p. 160).

The Marquis and Myers (1969) study of innovation in United States firms and the Carter and Williams (1957) study of British firms also support these findings. Table 3-4 summarizes both studies. It can be seen that the major sources of *ideas for* innovation came from marketing factors, as opposed to technological factors.

The foregoing studies thus indicate that in innovation the organization reacts to a need rather then being innovative in the sense of taking existing knowledge or means (i.e., technology) and trying to create a new need (i.e., output demand) whereby it can use its technology in a creative way.

It is also apparent from existing research that the sources of ideas for innovation come from outside the organization itself. In studying the 25 major process and product innovations in DuPont, Mueller (1962) indicated that 56% (14 cases) originated outside the organization. Marquis and Myers' (1969) analysis of 157 case studies of innovation has shown that 61% (96 cases) of the ideas for new innovations came from outside the organization. Utterback's (1971b study of innovation in the instrument industry found that of ". . . 59 pieces of information incorporated in the ideas for 32 new scientific and measuring instruments, 66% (39 pieces) came

Table 3-4. Sources of Successful Commercial Innovations

	Percentage of Innovations	
Source of Innovation	Carter and Williams	Myers and Marquis
Adopted (not original)	33	23
Technical factors; the desire to use the work of research- and-development departments	18	17
Marketing factors	32	35
Demands by customers for new types or qualities of product	12	
Direct pressure of competition (copying or forestalling rival/rms)	10	
Desire to meet excess demand	10	
Production factors	17	23
Desire to overcome labor shortage	5	
Desire to overcome materials shortage	12	
Administrative factors	n.a.	2
Total	100	100

(From Utterback, 1971 b:148)

SOURCES: Sumner Myers and D. G. Marquis, *Successful Commercial Innovations* (Washington, D.C.: National Science Foundation, 1969). Charles Carter and Bruce R. Williams, *Industry and Technical Progress: Factors Governing the Speed of Application of Science* (London: Oxford University Press, 1957).

from outside the firm that developed the idea" (Utterback, 1971, p. 145).

It can also be seen from Table 3-4 that both the Carter and Williams (1957) study (33%) and the Myers and Marquis' (1969) study (23%) indicate that a small percentage of innovations are adopted from outside the firm. Rather, the majority of innovations are developed, tested, marketed, or incorporated in existing operations by the firm itself. These findings do not contradict the preceding few pages where we have discussed how the sources of ideas and information concerning innovation come from outside the organization. Rather, it appears that innovative organizations need to be open to outside sources of information to get ideas for innovation before they then develop the innovations themselves. For example, Miller's (1971) study of 16 United States and Western European steel firms has also indicated that organizations do not innovate by the introduction of technology developed within their own organizations but rather by technology developed outside the firm. "Innovation behavior . . . follow(s) from a capacity to adapt and utilize technical possibilities offered by the environment, rather than from internal creativity" (Miller, 1971, p. 107).

Thus from the foregoing discussion it is evident that the interaction between the organization and its environment is crucial to the innovation process. The organization continually must obtain several kinds of information from the environment. *First*, it must determine the kinds of outputs the environment seeks that may require innovation to be more readily received by the environment. *Second*, it must discover the kinds of technology or means that may be required to produce the innovation—what are other organizations doing, are there existing innovations that the organization might adopt to facilitate its response to these needs? *Third*, once the organization does in fact implement the innovation, is the innovation effective in meeting the demands of the environment? Here it is necessary for the organization to get feed-back from the external environment.

This discussion also emphasizes the importance of the external environment in creating the impetus for innovation. For example, Terreberry's (1968) analysis of organizational environments has emphasized that ". . . changes in organizational environments are such as to increase the ratio of externally induced change to internally induced change" (pp. 591-592). However, in studying how organizations react to their external environment, it is important to focus on processes within the organization that facilitate the gathering and processing of information from the external environment. The essential variable in determining this is the organization's structure. In the following section, we focus on the role of organizational structure as it affects the innovation process.

ORGANIZATIONAL STRUCTURE AND INNOVATION

The major question to be addressed in this section is what type of organizational structure facilitates the process of innovation? We next briefly review some of the literature on organizational structure as it applies to the innovation process, then draw some conclusions concerning structure and innovation.

Characteristics of the Bureaucratic Organization [2]

The bureaucratic organization as initially specified by Weber (1947) has several distinct characteristics:

1. There is a hierarchy of authority in which each individual is accountable to his superior for his subordinates' decisions and actions as well as his own. This authority gives the

individual the right to issue directions to his subordinates, and they have the duty of obey these directives (Weber, 1947, p. 331).

2. There is a clear-cut division of labor among positions within the organization, which makes it possible for a high degree of specialization to develop (Weber, 1947, p. 331).

3. There is a system of rules and procedures developed that ensures the uniformity and continuity of the performance of tasks (Weber, 1947, p. 330).

4. Individuals carry out their tasks in an impersonal way, which prevents personal considerations from affecting their actions (Weber, 1947, p. 340; Blau, 1956, p. 30).

5. Employment within the organization is determined on the basis of technical qualifications and constitutes a career (Weber, 1947, p. 334).

From the Weberian perspective, then, the bureaucratic type of organization technically is, in this sense "capable of attaining the highest degree of effeciency and is in this formally the most rational known means of carrying out imperative control over human beings" (Weber, 1947, p. 337).

Weber has analyzed bureaucratic organizations as an ideal type rather than empirically. Thus this ideal-type conceptualization does not represent an average of all the attributes of existing bureaucratic organizations. Rather, it is derived as a pure type by abstracting the most characteristic bureaucratic aspects of organizations (Blau and Scott, 1962, p. 33).

Most contemporary organizational theorists argue that bureaucracy should be viewed as being dimensional and varying from one organization to another. Hall (1962) has considered six dimensions in his empirical assessment of bureaucracies. These dimensions are as follows:

1. A division of labor based on functional specialization.
2. A well defined hierarchy of authority.

3. A system of rules covering the rights and duties of positional incumbents.

4. A system of procedures for dealing with work situations.

5. Impersonality of interpersonal relations.

6. Promotion and selection for employment based upon technical competence (p. 33).

He found that bureaucratic characteristics are not highly intercorrelated; that is, ". . . organizations that are highly bureaucratized on any one dimension are not necessarily so on the other dimensions" (p. 34). Also, the presence of each dimension ranges along a continuum rather than existing in a present or absent dichotomy (p. 37).

Limitations of Bureaucratic Organization for Innovation

There have been a variety of criticisms of Weber's bureaucratic model, ranging from such issues as the failure to consider the informal organization (Blau, 1956) to the overspecification of rules (Selznick, 1949). However, in this discussion we focus on only those criticisms they relate specifically to reducing the capacity for the organization to innovate.

Monocratic Concept. One of the major problems of the bureaucratic model or organization, as Thompson (1969, pp. 15–16) has indicated, is its *monocratic* concept of the organization. This holds that (1) there is great inequality among organizational participants in their status, abilities, contributions to the organization, and rewards, (2) the organization's technology is simple and within the grasp of a few people, (3) the person at the top of the organization is assumed to be omniscient and issues all orders in the organization, (4) these orders are clarified downward by successive levels of subordinates, so that the delegation process is complete, (5) because there is only one source of legitimate authority in the organization, conflict is not seen as legitimate, and thus bargaining coalitions and other conflict-settling activities are illegitimate (Thompson, 1969, p. 16).

Thompson (1961, p. 6) has elaborated further on point three above in noting the growing gap and conflict between the right to decide (i.e., authority based on incumbency) and the ability to decide (i.e., authority based on technical competence.) This gap is increasing because of technological change, which leads to more specialization and occurs at a quicker rate than change in cultural definitions of hierarchial role (Thompson, 1961, p. 6). As a result of this, growing imbalance between rights of authority and ability and skills generates tensions and insecurities in the system and has a serious impact on the organization. These insecurities often translate themselves into (1) the need for control, (2) an exaggerated dependence upon regulations, (3) an exaggerated aloofness in interpersonal relations, and (4) an exaggerated resistance to change. Thompson (1961, pp. 152–177) refers to this syndrom as *bureaupathic behavior*.

Lack of Mechanisms for Dealing with Conflict. Various theorists have pointed out that an important characteristic of the innovation process in both individuals (Zaltman and Brooker, 1971; Rogers and Shoemaker, 1971) and organizations (Burns and Stalker, 1961; Wilson, 1966; Lynton, 1969) is dealing with conflict. Innovation and change involve changing the status quo. This often results in some conflict between those individuals who are striving for the innovation and those who are resisting the innovation.

Also, the creative process which is an important component of innovation operates best when there is a diversity among the individuals who are involved. Having a variety of individuals involved with different backgrounds is likely to bring more varied inputs into the creative process (Hoffman and Maier, 1961). Wilson (1966, p. 200) has hypothesized that the greater the diversity in the organization's task structure, the more likely innovations will be generated, because when the task structure is highly complex, it is harder to supervise individuals as closely, with the result that people have more freedom to innovate. However, given this heterogeneity in the individuals' background and their expectations, there is a greater likelihood that conflicts might develop.

March and Simon (1958, p. 153) have also indicated that complexity brings about conflict because the information received by individuals in one subunit is often different from that received by individuals in other subunits in the organization. The information sent to an individual in a specialized unit is filtered and structured according to the organizational location and professional orientation of the receiver. In a later section of this chapter we describe how organizations can deal with conflict and integrate more differentiated components.

The Overemphasis on Certainty. In discussing decision-making in Chapter 2 we criticized the rational-optimizing model for its emphasis on certainty and for specifying the necessity for considering all the alternatives and their consequences before the ultimate choice is made among the various alternatives. The more bureaucratic organization operates on this presumption of certainty in the decision environment. Organizational decision makers are assumed to know what they are looking for. Search is governed by the rule that it should continue until the margin cost of search begins to exceed the marginal improvement in alternatives found (March and Simon, 1958, p. 141). However, this rule is less applicable in innovation situations because decision makers are often less sure about exactly what they need. In many instances, the organization seeks innovation because of some immediate problem or crisis it faces. Often the organization has not dealt with the problem before so that uncertainty is high. Pre-established decision rules may be inappropriate, and new rules and procedures should be developed. Thus an important characteristic of the innovative organization is its ability to deal with uncertainty and exhibit instrumental innovations in its decision-making apparatus. For example, in his study of innovation in steel companies in the United States and Western Europe, Miller found that innovative organizations continually scan their environment to anticipate environmental variation and continually make incremental adjustments over time in their relations with the environment (Miller, 1971, p. 45). This continual adaption to changing uncertainty thus requires that the organization continually learn about the changing contingencies in the environment. For most organizations, especially those attempting to make some innovations, uncertainty is an important operating condition under which the organization functions.

In his criticism of the bureaucratic model, Litwak (1961) indicates that the organization will encounter some nonuniform events (i.e., uncertainty) for which it will be unable to preplan its course of action. The bureaucratic organization does not by design exclude nonuniform events from its concern. Rather, its emphasis on specific preplanning may result in rules or procedures that may hamper dealing with nonuniform, uncertain situations when they occur. For example, specific channels of communication may be specified that a manager is to use in communicating with the top hierarchy of the organization. However, the manager may experience some unexpected demand on his unit. He may not have enough time in responding to the new demand to go through normal channels to get information. If the rules in the organization are very specific concerning going through proper channels, the manager's capability to adapt to unexpected situations is limited.

Modified View of Organizational Structure

One of the major problems, then, with the bureaucratic model is the assumption that there is one best way to organize that applies to all situations the organization may encounter. This assumption is also problematical when discussing innovation, as the very bureaucratic type of structure may not be appropriate during the different initiation and implementation stages of the innovation process. In this section, we offer a somewhat modified view of organizational structure, then review some of the studies of innovation using this conceptualization.

Earlier in this chapter it was emphasized that an important function the organization must perform during the process of innovation is the gathering and processing of information from its environment. The organization's structure is seen here as the critical variable determining the effectiveness of the organization's information processing potential.

The Cybernetic Conception of Organization. The cybernetic conceptualization of organization as represented by Cadwallader (1959), Deutsch (1963), and Duncan (1973), is useful here in understanding the role of structure. It links the generalized concept of organization to that of information and communication. In this conceptualization a social system is a set of elements linked almost entirely by the intercommunication of information. The essential point here is that although the relations among components of mechanical systems are a function primarily of spatial and temporal considerations and the transmission of energy from one component to another, the interrelations among components in complex organizations depend more and more on the transmission of information. All social systems are communication networks held together by the flow of information. Miller (1965, p. 349) has also indicated that all subsystems are coordinated by information transmission and that systems also maintain their relationships with their environments by inputs and outputs of information. For example, in an organization the interrelations among the individuals and subgroups comprising it depend on the transmission of information about power and authority relationships, role demands, and whether current performance is meeting the organization's output requirements. If the information flow is not functioning properly, then there is likely to be ambiguity about power and authority relationships, role demands, and performance demands which may impede the interrelations among the components of the organization so that its effectiveness is less than optimal. For example, Kahn et al. (1964) found that when individuals experienced ambiguity concerning what was expected of them, they experienced job tension.

As indicated earlier in this chapter, the organization is viewed as an open system characterized by continual interaction with the environment and the necessity of perhaps having to change its structure to adapt to the environment. This critical capacity to persist through a change in structure is what general systems theorists call ultrastability (Cadwallader, 1969). Therefore, to further understand the innovation process in organizations, it is necessary to focus on these morphogenic processes that tend to elaborate or change the organization's structure as it innovates.

The Flexibility-Stability Dilemma. The organization must exhibit some flexibility as well as stability in its functioning, so that it can modify current practices to adapt to new situations when they arise. This requirement that the system be both flexible and stable can be mutually exclusive unless there is some form of compromise in these two strategies. Often the very process of developing stability into organizational functioning prevents the system from having the flexibility to adapt when situations change. Both Merton (1940) and Blau

(1960) have indicated how rules and procedures can become ends in themselves and thus prevent the system from adjusting to new unexpected situations when they arise. Chandler's (1962) historical analysis of industrial organizations has indicated the difficulties large corporations have in responding to changes in their environment. Often the necessary structural innovations could not be implemented in a given organization until there was a change in top management so that individuals untied to past practices could implement the innovations.

Thus these two requirements for stability and flexibility can be mutually exclusive. However, as Weick (1969, p. 39) has indicated, the organization can solve this stability-flexibility dilemma by alternating between flexibility and stability in its structuring of activities and simultaneously expressing these two forms in different parts of the organization. Thus the organization can be both flexible and stable.

For example, Shepard (1967) discusses how a military raiding unit during World War II used alternating forms.

> The planning before a raid was done jointly by the entire unit—the private having as much opportunity to contribute to the planning as the colonel. During the raid, the group operated under a strict military command system. Following each raid, the unit returned to the open system used in planning for purposes of evaluating and maximizing learning from each raid (pp. 474–475).

Contingency Theories of Organization. The implication from the foregoing is that there is no one best way to organize. Rather, there may be a variety of structural configurations that an organization might implement contingent on the type of situation the organization is facing. The rationale of this view is based on the communication net studies of Bavelas (1950), Guetzkow and Simon, (1955), and Guetzkow and Dill (1957). These small-group experiments found that highly centralized networks (one member has more channels and information than others) facilitate effective performance of routine problem solving. Networks that are low in centralization (all members share an equal number of channels and have access to the same amount of information) facilitate innovative nonroutine problem solving. (Collins and Guetzkow, 1964.)

Burns and Stalker (1961) were the first researchers to indicate that different types of organizational structures might be effective in different situations. Their study of technological innovation in the electronics industry identified two types of management or organizational structures that characterized the firms. The mechanistic structure is found in organizations operating under rather stable conditions, whereas the organic structure exists best under unstable conditions. The characteristics of these two organizational forms are presented in Table 3-5.

The organic system of management is better suited for rapidly changing environments and innovations of the reorientation type, because here the uncertainty and resulting information needs of the organization are likely to be high. From Table 3-5 it can be seen that the organic structure by its enhancment of greater participation of organization members in decision-making and communication processes is likely to facilitate the greater information gathering and processing needs of the organization.

Lawrence and Lorsch (1967a) found in a comparative study of six organizations operating in the same industrial environment that the sales, research, and production units within these organizations differed in their formal structure. They found that the production unit with a more certain subenvironment tends to have the highest structure, sales has the next highest degree of structure and fundamental research units which experienced the highest uncertainty have the least formal structure (Lawrence and Lorsch, 1967a, p. 18). The fundamental research group which is responsible for the initiation of innovations thus requires a different type of organizational structure from other segments of the organization that are important in the implementation phases of the innovation process.

Table 3-5. Mechanistic and Organic Organizational Forms

Mechanistic	Organic
1. Tasks are broken into very specialized abstract units	1. Tasks are broken down into subunits, but relation to total task of organization is much more clear
2. Tasks remain rigidly defined	2. There is adjustment and continued redefinition of tasks through interaction of organizational members
3. Specific definition of responsibility that is attached to individual's functional role only	3. Broader acceptance of responsibility and commitment to organization that goes beyond individual's functional role
4. Strict hierarchy of control and authority	4. Less hierarchy of control and authority sanctions derive more from presumed community of interest
5. Formal leader assumed to be omniscient in knowledge concerning all matters	5. Formal leader not assumed to be omniscient in knowledge concerning all matters
6. Communication is mainly vertical between superiors and subordinates	6. Communication is lateral between people of different ranks and resembles consultation rather than command
7. Content of communication is instructions and decisions issued by superiors	7. Content of communication is information and advice
8. Loyalty and obedience to organization and superiors is highly valued	8. Commitment to tasks and progress and expansion of the firm is highly valued
9. Importance and prestige attached to identification with organization itself	9. Importance and prestige attached to affiliations and expertise in larger environment

(Condensed from Burns and Stalker, 1961, pp. 119–122)

Duncan's (1973) study of decision groups in manufacturing and research and development organizations further elaborates on the notion of differentiation in organizational structure. Other organizational theorists such as the empirical work of Burns and Stalker (1961) and Lawrence and Lorsch (1967a) and the theoretical work of Litwak (1961) and Argyris (1964a) indicate that different parts of the organization may have different types of structures. Duncan's (1973) work shows that the *same* decision unit in the organization may implement different types of organizational structures at different points in time.

Structure is conceptualized and measured in terms of five dimensions: hierarchy of authority, degree of impersonality in decision making, degree of participation in decision making, degree of specific rules and procedures, and degree of division of labor. These dimensions constitute a decision-making structure. When these dimensions are highly structured, channels of communication and amount of information available within the unit are restricted. This is especially important when the environment is dynamic, the environmental uncertainty perceived is high, and a resulting high need exists for obtaining and processing new information. When dealing with high environmental uncertainty and change, a very high degree of emphasis on the hierarchy of authority can cause decision-unit members to adhere to specified channels of communication and selectively to feed back only positive information regarding their job. They would thus neglect any negative feedback that might actually help the organizational unit adapt better (Read, 1962). Strict emphasis on rigid rules, procedures, and division of labor may prohibit the unit from seeking new sources of information when new information inputs are required to adapt to the uncertainty of the environment, which may not have been foreseen when the rules and procedures were initially developed.

When the decision unit's environment is more certain,

however, the information demands on the decision unit are minimal, and it can respond more quickly to its environment by relying on pre-established rules and procedures, a well-specified division of labor, and so on. This more rigidly structured pyramidal decision-making structure is actually preferred over a loosely structured one (1) when time is of the essence, (2) in routine decision-making instances, (3) when environmental demands are clear and their implications are obvious, (4) when organizational circumstances approximate those of closed systems with minimal change requirements from the environment (see Thompson and Tuden, 1959; and Katz and Kahn, 1966).

The results of Duncan's (1973) study clearly demonstrates that decision-making units do alternate over time between flexibility and stability in structure in dealing with routine and nonroutine decisions, and that this is done in accordance with environmental changes or perceived environmental uncertainty. Decision units that experience high uncertainty (innovative situation) exhibit the greatest differences in their routine and nonroutine (innovative) decision-making structure, which is related to the decision units overall effectiveness. Thus when uncertainty is high the decision unit differentiates its decision-making procedures to deal with the information gathering and processing requirements that accompany high uncertainty.

In view of the sequential process model of Chapter 2, it should be stressed that what Duncan has termed a "nonroutine decision" under high environmental uncertainty is compatible with Harvey and Mills' (1970) notion of innovative situation; similarly, a routine decision is compatible with the notion of routine situation.

Duncan (1973) focuses on what in this book is termed the major stage of initiation in the innovation process; he identifies environmental conditions (in terms of perceived uncertainty) that require different structures of decision-making units. Shepard (1967) has also discussed the phenomenon of alternation; in this case, however, the alternation ("periodicity") takes place not within the initiation stage alone but between the initiation stage and implementation stage of the innovation process. For the former of these, Shepard says

. . . a quality of openness is needed so that diverse and heterogeneous persons can contribute, and so that many alternatives can be explored. For implementation, however, a quite different quality may be needed: singleness of purpose, functional division of labor, responsibility and authority, discipline, the drawing of internal communication boundaries, and so on (p. 474).

Coughlan et al.'s (1972) research on schools has also indicated that the decentralized collective decision structure may be used during the initiation stage of the innovation process to identify areas for innovation. Then the relatively centralized authority structure may be used during the implementation stage.

In this last section it has become apparent that there is no one best form for structuring organizations. Rather, we have suggested that it is more appropriate to view the structure of an organization as being comprised of a variety of dimensions that may vary from one situation to the next. We shall now discuss some of the specific characteristics of organizations as they relate to the innovation process.

Characteristics of Organizations as They Affect the Innovation Process

Complexity. The degree of complexity of the organization can have various effects on the innovation process. Complexity is defined here as the number of occupational specialties in the organization and their professionalism (Hage and Aiken, 1970, p. 33) with a very differentiated task structure (Wilson,

1966, p. 200). In a highly complex organization either its output or its technology (the process by which the output is produced) may not be highly specified. Thus as Wilson (·1966, p. 201) indicates, each individual has some latitude to tailor his task to fit his needs. Given the diverse nature in which individual tasks may be defined, it becomes very difficult for close supervision to occur. The supervisor may simply not be aware of the specific way each member has tailored his job. The result is that the individual has more of an opportunity to discover areas for innovation.

A high number of occupational specialties with professionalism results in organizational personnel placing high value on specific knowledge and information to utilize on the job. This diversity in occupational backgrounds can then bring a variety of sources of information to bear, which can facilitate awareness or knowledge of innovations at the initiation stage. These varied sources of information simply increase the opportunity for different types of information to be made available to the organization. For example, Peltz and Andrews (1966) found that scientific groups that have a wide diversity in academic background of their participants are more productive creatively. Also, these individuals with different occupational backgrounds performing different tasks bring different expectations on what the organization should be doing. The result is that there are likely to be performance gaps identified by some of the participants. However, because of differing expectations, there is likely to be more conflict about what should or should not be done (Burns and Stalker, 1961). Wilson (1966, pp. 200–204) has indicated that high diversity in the organization leads to organizational members conceiving and proposing more innovations but *not* adopting these innovations. Wilson's argument is that the high diversity (complexity) makes it difficult for any one source of authority to force some consensus toward agreement as to which of the many proposals should be implemented. Thus there appears to be a basic conflict between the search for the awareness of the innovation and implementation. This organizational dilemma is clearly exhibited in Sapolsky's (1967) study of innovation in department stores. The diversity in the reward structure in terms of increased professionalization on the part of retail controllers led to proposals to separate buying and selling functions, the use of computers in merchandising, and the use of sophisticated decision-making techniques such as PERT and operations research in merchandise problems. However, the diversity in department store's structural arrangements and decentralized decision-making authority and the existance of a large number of equally situated subunits frustrated the implementation of these proposed innovations (Sapolsky, 1967, p. 509). Carroll's (1967) study of innovation in medical schools also supports the idea that diversity in organizational units leads to innovation proposals, but that a more centralized authority is required to gain their actual acceptance and implementation into the organization.

However, Hage and Aiken's (1967) study of program change in 16 social welfare organizations is somewhat contradictory to these findings. They found reasonably strong correlations between measures of complexity (number of occupational specialties r equal to .48, amount of extra-organizational professional activity r equal to .37, and amount of professional training r equal to .14) *and the actual adoption* of new programs or services in these social welfare organizations. However, they did find a negative relationship (r equal to minus .17) between rate of program change and expressive relations because of the possible conflicts that occupational diversity may create.

Their study does not specifically examine mechanisms for integrating highly diverse groups and reducing conflict between them. However, it may be that these mechanisms help highly complex organizations not only initiate innovations but also implement them. This view is consistent with

Lawrence and Lorsch's (1967a, p. 30) study which found that effective highly diverse organizations have specific subsystems whose major function is to serve as integrative units both to coordinate and deal with the conflict between the highly diverse units. We discuss in a later section of this chapter the specific mechanisms for dealing with conflict.

Cooke [3] has offered a somewhat different explanation for the positive relationship in Hage and Aiken's (1967) study between complexity and the adoption of innovations. High complexity radically increases the number of innovations proposed or initiated in an organization. On the other hand, low complexity facilitates the implementation of the innovations. According to Cooke, this implies that many innovations initiated in a complex organization are never implemented, whereas a greater proportion of innovations in less-complex organizations are initiated within those systems. However, the positive relationship between complexity and initiation is possibly greater than the negative complexity and implementation relationship. Thus complex organizations may actually implement a greater number of innovations simply as a result of more being initiated.

In any event, from the foregoing discussion it appears that the complexity of the organization can have both positive and potentially negative effects on various stages of the innovation process. At the *initiation* stage, highly diverse organizations apparently are able to bring a variety of bases of information and knowledge to bear that can increase the awareness and knowledge of innovations and general proposals for innovation. However, at the *implementation* stage high complexity, because of potential conflicts, makes it more difficult for the organization to actually implement the innovation.

The strategy implications for the practitioner concerning the complexity dilemma are several. First, the diversity of an organization or subgroup of an organization might be increased to increase the number of innovations proposed during the initiation stage. For example, a project group might be composed of several engineers, production managers, and marketing managers to develop new product innovations. The heterogenous background of this group with its diverse sources of information could generate many new proposals. To facilitate the selection of several proposals for implementation, team-building activities could be provided. Team building would help the project group develop their interpersonal skills and trust so that they could openly deal with the conflict and disagreements they would experience in trying to implement certain innovation proposals. (Beckhard, 1969).

Second, the highly creative initiation stage of the innovation process might be once again carried out by a highly complex group with individuals with very diverse backgrounds. Then the various innovation proposals might be presented to a different, less-complex unit that would select a given proposal for implementation. For example, a highly diverse research-and-development unit might generate certain innovation proposals for changing the production process in an organization. These various proposals could then be presented to the less-diverse manufacturing division, which because of greater potential consensus in how they view their task, could more quickly and with less conflict select a proposal for implementation.

Formalization. By formalization we mean the emphasis placed within the organization on following specific rules and procedures in performing one's job. The assumption is that strict emphasis on rigid rules and procedures may prohibit organizational decision makers from seeking new sources of information. Thus there is simply less opportunity for them to become more aware of potential innovations or to identify performance gaps in terms of how the organization is doing.

In some instances, performance gaps might be identified between what the organization or subunit is doing and what participants perceive it should be doing, but the rules and procedures specified by the organization prevent the decision makers from taking corrective action. The end result is that the individuals involved experience some role conflict. They are expected both to meet the role expectation of reducing performance gaps when they occur and to do this according to the rules and procedures specified by the organization.

A classic example of this is the situation where an assembly-line foreman, in trying to meet increased quality control demands on his line, must make modifications in some of the components of the final product. The specific rules and procedures may state that when modifications are needed in component parts, this request should be sent in writing to the engineering department, which evaluates it and then sends instructions to those departments making the component. However, the assembly-line foreman may be under such time pressures to make the quality improvements because of increased output demands that he has his own department make the modifications in the component part. Thus to reduce the performance gap the individual has to violate some of the specific rules and procedures that have been set up in the organization. The individual is thus likely to experience some role conflict and resulting pressure and stress (Kahn et al., 1964).

In discussing the relationship between formalization and innovation it is again necessary to consider the particular stage of the innovation process. For example, Shepard (1967, p. 474) has indicated that low formalization might be most appropriate at the initiation phase, whereas a higher degree of formalization may be more appropriate during the implementation phase. During the *initiation* stage the organization needs to be as flexible and as open as possible to new sources of information and alternative courses of action. Many rules and procedures might become restraints under which the organization must operate. This seems to be the case that Hage and Aiken's (1967, p. 511) study of welfare organizations makes in finding a negative relationship (r equal to minus .47 between job codification and program change.

During the *implementation* stage, Shepard (1967, p. 474) indicates that a singleness of purpose is required. In order to bring the innovation into practice, Neal and Radnor's (1971) study of the successful implementation of operation research-management science activities in large industrial organizations indicates ". . . significantly strong positive relationships between the establishment of an overall policy and procedural guidelines and the success of the OR/MS group" (p. 22). In another study of the formalization process in OR/MS, Radnor and Neal (1971) found that in 108 large industrial firms, studied in 1968 and again in 1970, specific procedures had been established for implementation. They found that in the 2 years that passed, the makeup of OR/MS personnel changed from primarily professional scientists or OR/MS specialists (people with specific training in OR/MS prior to coming to business organizations) to organizational men (people who moved through the organization and later moved into OR/MS positions) (Radnor and Neal, 1971, pp. 4–6). The result was that among OR/MS personnel there was a more organizational orientation—they had a better understanding of the organization's needs and thus attempted more realistic and useful applications.

They also found that other specific formalized procedures had been developed to facilitate implementation. These procedures cover such factors as formal project selection, long-range planning, scheduling, and regular progress reports (Radnor and Neal, 1971, p. 19). The formalization procedures appear to have reduced the problems of implementing OR/MS activities. Apparently, the formalized procedures they identified provide both information and specific techniques that facilitate the organizational personnel's ability to utilize the innovation. The lack of these more-formalized procedures at the implementation stage is likely to lead to both role conflict and role ambiguity. Role ambiguity could result because without more formal procedures the individual is likely to be unclear concerning how the innovation is to be implemented and how this new innovation will affect how he performs his job. Role conflict could also occur, because the lack of specific procedures concerning how the innovation will be implemented may lead to conflict with existing rules and procedures.

For example, a new, more centralized management information system might be introduced into an organization. Previously, information channels may have been decentralized and informal, with the information system fairly unstructured. The new information system is thus a significant change from the old one. To be successfully implemented, it would be necessary for quite specific procedures to be communicated to personnel, so that they could know that they are now expected to utilize the more-centralized communication system. They are thus made aware that the role expectations their superiors have for them concerning the information system have changed, and that the older, informal, decentralized system is no longer sanctioned.

Gross et al.'s (1971) study of the attempted implementation of a new teacher role model illustrates the problem that role ambiguity and conflict can create. The attempted innovation, the catalytic role model, was an attempt to help teachers deal with motivational problems of lower-class children (Gross et al., 1971, p. 10). In analyzing some of the barriers to the implementation of the innovation, teachers indicated that they were not clear about the kinds of role performance that were required to carry out the innovation (i.e., role ambiguity was high). Also, there were incompatible organizational arrangements that did not support the new teacher model innovation (pp. 139–142). The new teacher model focused on the process of learning, whereas during the time of attempted implementation teachers were still required to give grades. Also, creating classrooms with students of various ages was an important part of the new teaching model. However, during the attempted implementation, classrooms were homogenously formed on the basis of age. Thus in both instances the teachers experienced role conflict that lead to the abandonment of the innovation.

Thus we again find that the effect of the degree of formalization varies depending on the stage of the innovation process the organization is in. At the initiation stage it appears that less formalization, in terms of specific rules and procedures, provides a more open system to gather and process information, which is likely to increase knowledge awareness of innovations. However, at the implementation stage, it seems that more-specific rules and procedures can facilitate changing the organizational role member's expectations and role demands so that the innovation can be utilized.

Once again the practitioner is faced with a dilemma—low formalization seems to facilitate the initiation stage of innovation, whereas higher formalization appears to aid the implementation of innovations. In attempting to reduce this dilemma the organization might use different degrees of formalization at the initiation and implementation stages of innovation. For example, a broad set of operating guidelines might be established for a group to reduce formalization during the initiation phase of the innovation process, which as indicated above would potentially stimulate innovation proposals. However, once the proposals are generated the group could then focus on specifying operating rules and procedures on how the innovation would actually be implemented. This more formalized innovation process at the implementation stage would tend to reduce the ambiguity and potential conflict that individuals can experience as they implement the innovation. They potentially would have a better understanding of how to use the innovation and how its implementation fits into existing procedures in the organization.

Centralization. The centralization dimension is conceptualized here in terms of the locus of the authority and decision making in the organization. The greater the hierarchy of authority (the higher in the organization decision making takes place) and less participation in decision making that exists in the organization, the greater the centralization and vice versa. In discussing the innovation process in organizations we have emphasized the role uncertainty plays. Earlier, we indicated that during the process of innovation a good deal of uncertainty may be experienced by organizational members at the initiation stage. Some performance gap may have been identified in the organization, and thus there is increased search for alternative courses of action. Here, as we have indicated, the information needs for the organization are very high. A very high degree of hierarchy of authority is likely to restrict the channels of communication and reduce the amount of information available to the organization.

A strict emphasis on hierarchy of authority often causes decision unit members to adhere to specified channels of communication and selectively to feed back only positive information regarding their job. They thus neglect any negative feedback which might actually help the organization better innovate (Read, 1962). Also, Shepard (1967, p. 471) has pointed out that the ideas for innovation are often generated at some distance from the power center in the organization, thus they must be communicated up the hierarchy. The more bureaucratized the authority structure, the more channels of communication the innovation has to travel through. This, then, increases the probability that the proposal may get screened out, because it violates the status quo in the organization. As Thompson (1969) has indicated, in a centralized, more-bureaucratized organization, it is simply easier for the idea for the innovation to get vetoed.

Greater participation in decision making may bring new insights to bear and new sources of information to the innovation process. More participation in the decision-making process can also increase organizational members' commitment to working through the sometimes difficult implementation stage, with the result that resistance is reduced (Marrow et al., 1967).

Hage and Aiken's (1967, pp. 510–511) study of welfare organizations found that there is a positive relationship (r equal to .49) between participation in decision making and the rate of program change. They also found a negative relationship (r equal to minus .09) between hierarchy of authority and program change. Burns and Stalker's (1961) study indicated that the organic structure, with its smaller hierarchy of authority and wider involvement in decision making, is more effective in dealing with the more unstable (i.e., uncertain) conditions that often accompany attempts of innovation. Lawrence and Lorsch's (1967a) study also found that fundamental research units, as a result of the greater uncertainty they face, exhibit less structure than production units.

Although the available research is less clear on this, we suggest once again that the effects of centralization can vary, depending on the stage of the innovation process the organization is in. It is clear that a smaller hierarchy of authority and more participation in decision making can increase the information available to the organization and thus increase knowledge awareness of innovations at the initiation stage. However, as Shepard (1967) has indicated, when the organization gets to the implementation stage, a more specific line of authority and responsibility is required. Blau and Scott (1962, p. 125) have also noted that the hierarchical differentiation by status curbs the free flow of ideas and thus facilitates the coordination of opinions to achieve consensus. Also clear lines of authority facilitate members' knowing what is expected of them regarding the innovation. Thus role conflict and ambiguity can be reduced.

We might again look at the results of Lawrence and Lorsch's (1967a) study as support for the argument that centralization can have various effects on the innovation process. They (p. 18) found that in effective organizations the fundamental research groups have the least structure, whereas the production units are most structured. Although Lawrence and Lorsch did not discuss this, it may be that the fundamental research units are most responsible for the initiation stage of the innovation process. They explore alternative courses of action that the organization might follow. They are continually scanning the environment for new opportunities. Here a very flexible organizational structure is most appropriate for gathering and processing the information needed for decision making. However, as the organization moves to the implementation stage of producing the product with whatever innovations are made, it becomes important to implement much clearer lines of authority so that personnel know what is expected of them. Thus production units, where the innovations are implemented, are more centralized. As indicated earlier, Wilson (1966) points out that when authority and structure are diverse, it becomes difficult for the organization to gather enough influence over participants. Sapolsky's (1967) study of innovation in department stores found that decentralized authority and decision-making structures frustrate attempts to implement the innovations.

Also, with authority and power more diffused among organizational members, more conflict and opposition to the innovation are likely to occur because participants may perceive that the innovation could reduce the amount of influence they currently have. Also, Corwin (1969) and Gamson (1966) have indicated that the more decentralized the decision process, the greater the opportunity for different groups and individuals to express disagreement. Participation provides an opportunity and channel for discontented individuals to communicate grievances that might otherwise remain unknown (Corwin 1969, p. 509).

Once again it appears that centralization can have different effects at different stages of the innovation process. Less centralization appears to be more appropriate in gathering and processing the information at the initiation stage. Here less emphasis on hierarchy of authority and more participation in decision making is likely to increase the information available and thus facilitate the awareness of innovations. However, at the implementation stage it may be that more strict channels of authority can reduce potential conflict and ambiguity that could impair implementation. Again the strategy for the organization may be to utilize more-decentralized procedures during the initiation stage and then more-centralized procedures during implementation stage. The organization thus needs to implement different types of decision structures during the different phases of the innovation process.

Interpersonal Relations. Traditional theories of organization (Weber 1947) have indicated that there should be high impersonality in interpersonal relations among organizational participants to maintain a high emphasis on rationality in the organization. Argyris (1962) has summarized the values implicit in formal organizations concerning interpersonal relationships: "Effectiveness in human relationships increases as behavior is rational, logical and clearly communicated. Effectiveness decreases as emotionality increases" (p. 39). Argyris suggests that we focus on interpersonal relations as they affect the decision-making process in organizations.

An orientation toward dealing with interpersonal issues may be important in the innovation process. In innovation situations, organizational participants face uncertainty, and strategies for dealing with these situations usually have not been covered by pre-established rules and procedures. Here greater reliance must be placed on the informal network of relationships. For example, Conrath (1968) has studied informal groups in research-and-development organizations and has pointed out that these informal groups provide important sources of information to the formal hierarchy.

Also, during the uncertainty and risk taking that often take place during the innovation process, organizational participants may experience stress and anxiety. Torrance's (1961) and Schroder, Driver and Streufert's (1967) research on stress indicates that continued stress within the group destroys communication linkages and reduces the group's level of performance. If individuals are fully integrated into the group, information-processing capabilities are potentially increased by the individual's commitment to working toward group goals.

Dealing with interpersonal issues also seems to be important, because of the effects of good interpersonal skills on openness, risk taking, and trust, which are important components of the innovation process. Argyris' (1965) work points out that when individuals do not own up to their own behavior or are not open to the effects of their behavior on others, those around them are less likely to take risks and are more likely to conform in their behavior. This obviously deters the innovation process at all stages. For example, Stephenson et al.'s (1971) study of creative research-and-development laboratories found that creative labs were ones ". . . in which people are willing to take chances with their personal reputations . . . to defend ideas that may be unpopular . . . to take chances by being open and honest with fellow workers" (p. 47). Argyris notes that managers need to change their values concerning interpersonal relations to include that view that: "Human relationships increase in effectiveness as all the relevant behavior (rational and interpersonal) becomes conscious, discussable, and controllable" (Argyris, 1964b, p. 61).

It is important to place the emphasis on interpersonal relations as specified by Argyris in perspective with the need for rational behavior in organizations. Whyte (1969) probably summarizes this better than anyone:

> The Argyris prescription . . . is not a substitution of emotionalism for technical, rational discussion. He advocates what he calls "openness" or "authenticity," which is his particular combination of rational and emotional communication. Openness does not mean that each individual should express whatever is on his mind regardless of any concern for the feelings of others. The aim is to create a situation in which the members of an organization who are working closely together can each express how they feel about problems in their relationships in such a manner as to help those with whom they are communicating to express themselves in a similar open manner. The theory is that the emotional problems within the group do not simply disappear when they are not faced by members of the group; rather they tend to obstruct the carrying out of the rational plans of the members. The theory holds further that the technical problems can be more effectively resolved if emotional problems are not suppressed but are dealt with along with a development of rational plans (p. 391).

It is less clear how dealing with interpersonal relations might effectively vary during the different steps of the innovation process. It may well be, given the preceding arguments, that it is important that the organization deal with interpersonal issues during all phases of the process of innovation.

Ability to Deal with Conflict. At various points in our discussion it has been emphasized that conflict is likely to appear during various stages of the innovation process. During the initiation stage conflicts can arise concerning what innovation proposals should be accepted and preserved. During the implementation stage, there are also likely to be conflicts about the process by which the innovation is to be integrated into the organization's ongoing practice.

The structural characteristics of innovative organizations can have a high potential for intraorganizational conflict. Table 3-6 summarizes the major structural antecedents to conflict. From Table 6 it can be seen that conflict occurs quite frequently during the stages of innovation.

For example, during the innovation process, organizational units are likely to feel some need for joint decision making as well as have some differences in their goals. As the

Table 3-6. Summary of Structural Antecedents to Interorganizational Conflict

I. Felt need for joint decision making which is function of (March and Simon, 1958; Walton et al., 1969):
  A. Mutual dependence on limited resources
  B. Interdependence of timing of activities

II. Differences in goals which may be function of:
  A. Ambiguity of goals (Walton et al., 1969)
  B. Organizational reward systems that place groups in competition for scarce resources (March and Simon, 1958; Blake et al., 1964; Walton et al., 1969)
  C. Perception of greater conflicts of interests between units (Walton et al., 1969)

III. Differences in perception of reality which may be function of:
  A. The number of independent information sources (March and Simon, 1958)
  B. Limiting the number of organizational members to whom any given bit of information is transmitted (March and Simon, 1958)
  C. Physical obstacles to communication (Walton et al., 1969)
  D. Higher the specialization of organization (Corwin, 1969)

IV. Higher the number of levels of authority (Corwin, 1969; Harvey and Mills, 1970)

V. Greater the complexity of the organization (Wilson, 1966; Corwin, 1969)

VI. Greater the emphasis on standardization of procedures, emphasis on rules, and close supervision (Corwin, 1969) initiation stage of innovation takes place in the research division of the organization, production people often feel that they should have some input to the decision-making process so that the innovation is compatible with existing production techniques. For example, Lawrence and Lorsch (1967a) found that the research units in organizations had very different goals (innovative products) than production units (low manufacturing costs) which resulted in the former having a much longer time horizon in task completion. Thus there are likely to be some disagreements between the research personnel and the production personnel.

Lawrence and Lorsch (1967b) found that in the highly diverse organizations they studied those that were more effective had specific formalized units established to integrate the diverse groups. These integrators help coordinate the diverse units and reduce conflicts that might occur. They found that effective integrators have several characteristics. (1) Effective integrators are influential because of their knowledge and expertise, in addition to just having a formal power base. If the integrator has prior experience in two or more of the different functional areas he is trying to help coordinate, he will be even more effective because he will be perceived as very competent. (2) The effective integrator has a balanced orientation between the departments he is attempting to integrate. The integrator speaks the language of each of the different departments. For example, he falls between the highly social-oriented behavior patterns of the sales group and the task-oriented behavior of the production unit. The integrator shares more behavior and thought patterns with the different managers than the managers do with each other. (Lawrence and Lorsch 1967b, p. 147) (3) Effective integrators also use a particular strategy of confronting conflict. Confrontation "involves placing all relevant facts before the disputants and then discussing the basis of disagreement until some alternative is found that provides the best solution for the total organization" (Lawrence and Lorsch 1967b, p. 149). They found this strategy much more effective in dealing with conflict than trying to force the resolution of the conflict or smooth it over. (4) They also found that effective integrators, as opposed to ineffective integrators, have certain preferred behavioral styles: they prefer to take significantly more initiative and leadership; they are more ambitious, active, and forceful; they have more poise in social situations and are more imaginative and spontaneous; they prefer more flexible ways of acting. (Lawrence and Lorsch 1967b, p. 150).

There are various other types of conflicts that might exist in organizations in addition to the *interperson-intergroup conflict* indicated above (Derr, 1972). It is important to indicate these, as well as strategies for resolving them. *Intrapersonal conflict* occurs between an individual and the organization. The individual's needs are not compatible with the demands the organization makes. A scientist in an organization has certain needs to be creative. However, he may be required to work on projects that are more practical and do not allow him to utilize his skills. Thus he experiences some conflict. *Organizational conflict* occurs as a direct result of organizational actions. For example, a budget cut in a system might increase competition and conflict between functional groups as they compete for scarce resources. This type of conflict cannot be reduced by improving relations between individuals or groups. Rather, changes must be made at the organizational level (Derr, 1972). In the budget example, the organization would need to reconsider the allocation of scarce resources. *Interorganizational conflict* is the conflict between competing organizations or internal subsystems acting if they are a separate organization (Derr, 1972). He indicates that in this type of conflict participants want to take ". . . economic resources, legitimate authority, popular support, the symbols of power, and other resources that are scarce . . ." (1972, p. 497). The most extreme type of con-

Table 3-7. Organizational Conflict Resolution Grid

Nature of the Conflict	Training Programs			Organizational Interventions		
	Knowledge	Simulated Experiences	Structure	Procedures	Norms	Remove the Causes
Intrapersonal	Organizational psychology (counseling and coaching)	T-groups, role plays, cases, the expectations survey	Counselors and staff development programs	Improve recruiting so as to not raise false expectations, counseling, role negotiation	Being sensitive, understanding the other's point of view	
Interpersonal	Group dynamics	Role plays, practicing open disagreement of differences, imaging, hand mirroring	Third-person consultants, integrators	Improve communication skills, problem-solving techniques, contract setting, selfish bargaining	Openness, confrontive climate, accepting conflict as natural	
Organizational	Organizational design, role theory	"Power game," * the influence line, the hollow square puzzle, the confrontation meeting	An effective structure and top management group	Role negotiation, fair mechanisms for resource allocation and personal advancement	OK to act in one's own self-interest, feeling free to air grievances, legitimize	

					questioning authority and policies
Interorganizational	Bargaining or negotiation strategies	"Disarmament game," † cases	Negotiating team	Work on negotiation agendas, prepare for future demands, work on tactics	Accepting the negotiation process as normal, equal power of groups, being tactical and cool
Revolutionary	Revolutionary tactics	"M.I.T. community game," ‡ cases	Persons in constant contact with dissident groups	Prepare forces for the attack, work to resolve basic problems, appeal to middle-of-the-roaders	Not taking attacks personally, thinking tactically, not over-reacting, offense as well as defense

(From Derr, 1972, p. 499)

* Power game brings out organizational conflicts.
† Disarmament game focuses on negotiation.
‡ MIT community game focuses on problems of revolutionary change.

flict is *revolutionary conflict.* Here the demand is for all the resources to be distributed to the formation of a new organization (Derr, 1972, p. 497).

Derr (1972, p. 498) indicates that these organizational conflicts can be resolved by (1) training managers to resolve conflict, (2) organizational development personnel making various interventions, (3) removing the causes of the conflict. His organizational conflict resolution grid is presented in Table 3-7.

From the foregoing discussion it can be seen that there are certain strategies the organization can use to reduce conflict. We have focused on conflict that occurs as a result of the innovation, as well as other organizational issues. The main objective here is to present the reader with a broad view of the sources of conflict as well as potential strategies for resolution.

SUMMARY

The role of the environment as it affects the innovation process is discussed in the first part of this chapter. Components of the environment are identified, as is the fact that organizations seem to get ideas and information about their innovations from sources external to the organization. However, once the idea for the innovation is obtained, the majority of innovations are developed, tested, marketed, or incorporated in the existing operations by the firm itself. Thus it appears that innovative organizations need to be open to outside sources of information to get ideas for innovations before they then develop innovations themselves.

In the second part of the chapter a multidimensional view of organization structure is presented. This model specifies that different configurations of organizational structure facilitate the innovation processes in its different stages. Specifically it is emphasized that in stimulating the initiation of innovations, a higher degree of complexity, lower formalization, and lower centralization facilitate the gathering and processing of information, which is crucial to the initiation stage. It is also emphasized that in the implementation stage a higher level of formalization and centralization and a lower level of complexity are likely to reduce role conflict and ambiguity, which could impair implementation. This conclusion thus implies that the organization must shift its structure as it moves through the various stages of innovation; at the earlier initiation stage a more-organic or less-bureaucratic structure seems most appropriate. Then, as the organization moves to the implementation stage, more-bureaucratic structure becomes appropriate.

Also, the organization needs to develop integrative conflict-reducing mechanisms to deal with the more differentiated organizational structure.

What clearly is needed now is for more systematic research to be done to monitor the various stages of the innovation process in organizations. This research would generate more information concerning how managers could actively facilitate the innovation process by implementing different changes in the organizations' structure.

NOTES

1. For a more complete discussion of organizational environments, see Duncan (1972a). The following discussion is based on this paper.
2. For an excellent discussion of the concept of bureaucracy, see Perrow (1972).
3. Personal communication from Robert Cooke.

4 Theories of Innovation in Organizations

CONTENTS

INTRODUCTION

This chapter consists of a short review of the theory of innovation in organizations presented in the book and a brief
review of some selected theories. However, again it is important to distinguish between innovation and organizational
change. Innovation is any idea, practice, or material artifact
perceived to be new by the relevant unit of adoption. The innovation, then, is the change object. Change, on the other
hand, is the alteration in the structure and functioning of a
social system. All innovations imply change. Not all change
involves innovations since not everything an organization
adopts is perceived as new.

REVIEW OF THE ZALTMAN, DUNCAN,
HOLBEK THEORY

The theory in this book has focused on the innovation process at the level of the organization. The initiation and implementation stages of the innovation process, identified and discussed in Chapter 2, are presented in Table 4-1.

The characteristics of the organization as they affect the
innovation process are noted in Chapter 3. Table 4-2 is a

Table 4-1.   Stages of Innovation-
Adoption Process

I. Initiation stage
  1. Knowledge-awareness substage
  2. Formation of attitudes toward
     innovation substage
  3. Decision substage

II. Implementation stage
  1. Initial implementation
  2. Continued-sustained implementation

Table 4-2. Structural Variables and Mediating Factors Affecting the Initiation and Implementation of Innovations

Initiation Stage	Mediators	Implementation Stage
Higher complexity	High capability for effective interpersonal relations	Lower complexity
Lower formalization	High capability for dealing with conflict	Higher formalization
Lower centralization		Higher centralization

summary of organizational characteristics facilitating the initiation and implementation stages of the innovation adoption process. As pointed out in Chapter 3 the organizational variables of effective interpersonal relationships and conflict resolution capabilities are mediators in the organization's being able to differentiate its degree of complexity, formalization, and centralization in the initiation and implementation stages of innovation. Therefore, the two mediating factors between the initiation and implementation stages are also introduced in this table. (1) It is important to note the innovation dilemma involved: the desirable degree of organizational complexity, formalization, and centralization that facilitates initiation is opposite those desirable in magnitude and direction to be operative during the implementation stage. These factors are reviewed briefly here with a discussion of some specific strategies the practitioner might use to lessen this dilemma.

Complexity

As indicated in Chapter 3, the greater complexity (e.g., number of occupational specialities, their professionalism and differentiated task structure) of the organization provides the opportunity to bring more-varied kinds of information to bear on decision situations. This increase in information can identify more innovation proposals. However, high complexity, because of potential conflicts and the difficulties in reaching consensus as to what innovations to implement, can make implementation difficult.

Several strategies have been suggested to reduce the innovation dilemma with respect to complexity. For example, (1) team-building activities could be provided to the highly complex group to help them develop their interpersonal skills and trust so that they can deal openly with conflicts and disagreements they might experience in trying to implement some subset of innovation proposals (French and Bell, 1973, pp. 112–121); (2) the highly complex unit might generate the innovation proposals, then let a less complex unit select the innovations to be implemented. A research-and-development unit might generate various innovative proposals for changing the assembly line in a production unit. Once these proposals are identified, the less complex production unit can select the proposal for implementation.

Formalization

Formalization focuses on the emphasis on following specific rules and procedures in the organization. During initiation strict emphasis on rules and procedures might inhibit organizational decision makers from seeking new sources of information because existing procedures might be quite rigid in specifying both the appropriate sources of information and channels of communication. There would thus be less opportunity for participants to become more aware of potential innovations or to identify performance gaps in terms of how the organization is doing. However, during implementation more clearly specified rules and procedures can facilitate implementation by reducing the ambiguity concerning how the individual's job is affected by the innovation.

To reduce the innovation dilemma here the organization can use different degrees of formalization at the initiation and implementation stages. During initiation a broad set of operating guidelines could be established that reduce formalization and give individuals more autonomy in seeking solutions to decision problems. Then, when the proposals are generated, the group can specify operating rules and procedures on how the innovation is to be implemented. This may reduce the potential ambiguity surrounding the implementation of the innovation.

Centralization

Centralization focuses on the locus of authority and decision making in the organization. The higher the level in the organization decisions are made and the less participation that exists in decision making, the more the centralization. At the initiation stage less emphasis on hierarchy of authority and more participation in decision making should increase the information available and, therefore, facilitate the awareness of innovations. During the implementation stage stricter channels of authority can reduce potential conflict and ambiguity that may impair implementation.

Once again the strategy for reducing the innovation dilemma is to utilize different degrees of centralization during the different stages of innovation. During initiation more autonomy can be given to participants to facilitate the awareness and knowledge of innovations. Then during the implementation stage the decision process would become more coordinated and centralized as specific innovations are selected for implementation. This would again have the potential for reducing the ambiguity associated with implementation.

Interpersonal Relations

Table 4-2 indicates that interpersonal relationships are important as a mediating variable linked to both major stages of the innovation process. During initiation, where uncertainty may be high, greater emphasis may have to be placed on informal relationships. Conrath's (1968) work has indicated that informal groups in research-and-development organizations provide important sources of information. Also, the ability to deal with relationship problems between individuals that may occur during both initiation and implementation is important. The point here is that "technical problems can be more effectively resolved if emotional problems are not suppressed but are dealt with along with a development of rational plans" (Whyte, 1969, p. 391).

Dealing with Conflict

Table 4-2 also indicates that the ability to deal with conflict is an important mediating variable. During initiation there will be conflicts concerning what innovation proposals should be accepted. The manner in which the conflict is resolved affects implementation processes. There also will be conflicts about the processes by which the innovation is to be integrated into the organization's ongoing practice. Legitimizing conflict as a likely occurrence during the innovation process and as something that should be confronted can facilitate innovation. Confrontation involves placing the relevant facts before the parties involved, then discussing the disputed issues until some agreement is found. Confronting the conflict can reduce the basis of disagreement and facilitate the opportunity for consensus to occur on what types of innovation proposals should be brought forth and what proposals will be selected for implementation.

ATTRIBUTES OF INNOVATIONS AND SUBSTAGES IN ADOPTION

The model advocated here appears to be somewhat more sensitive to the nature of innovations than are the other models. That is, the model better enables the researcher and manager to take into account the differential significance of the attributes of the innovation in question. The various attributes can be classified according to the particular substage in which their influence is most likely to be present. This does not mean, of course, that a given attribute is relevant at only one stage. For that matter, not all attributes of innovations discussed in Chapter 1 are relevant for all innovations. It is postulated here that at the knowledge-awareness substage such attributes as communicability, gatekeeper, and point of origin are likely to be important. For example, the more communicable an innovation is, the greater the chance that relevant information will be disseminated and therefore the greater the chance of establishing knowledge awareness among the potential adopters. At the attitude-formation substage, status quo ante, social cost, risk and uncertainty, compatibility, and complexity are likely to be perceived as the important factors. For example, the more compatible the innovation is with existing value and belief systems within the organization, the more readily favorable attitudes will be formed. The decision substage involves perceived relative advantage, scientific status, and financial cost. The long-run financial obligations, for example, incurred in the adoption of new equipment whose maintenance requirements may not be known is a factor in the decision stage. At the initial-implementation stage impact on interpersonal relationships are likely to be considered important, as well as the issue of terminality. The continued-sustained implementation substage probably involves the gateway capacity of innovations and its susceptibility to successive modification. These are presented in Table 4-3.

Table 4-3. Probable Interaction of Attributes with Innovation Process Substances

Attributes of Innovations	Decision Stages				
	Knowledge	Attitude Formation	Decision	Initial Implementation	Sustained Implementation
Cost		X	X		
Returns to investment		X			
Efficiency		X			
Risk and uncertainty		X			
Communicability	X				
Compatibility		X			
Complexity		X			
Scientific status			X		
Perceived relative advantage			X		
Point of origin	X				
Terminality				X	
Status quo ante		X			
Commitment			X		
Interpersonal relationships				X	
Public versus private				X	
Gatekeeper	X				
Susceptibility to successive modification					X
Gateway capacity					X
Gateway innovation					X

The preceding linkage of innovation attributes with the adoption substages shown in Table 4-3 is only suggestive. The particular problem and proposed solution(s), the nature of the organization, and the general context in which change is to occur are all factors in determining which particular attributes are most salient at various substages. The important point is that the various attributes of innovations should be considered in light of the substages in which they are likely to be most important. It is felt that the two-stage–five-substage model advocated in this book is especially amenable to this activity. It is also important to consider the interaction between the various types of innovations (ultimate/instrumental, programmed/nonprogrammed, and routine/radical) and the various substages. Different substages may be differentially important in the different types of innovations. For example, the decision substage may be relatively more important for radical innovations than for routine innovations. Greater deliberations are required to decide on complex aspects of the innovation as it affects the organization.

In Chapter 2 the topic of resistance to change is discussed at the organizational and individual level. This is summarized here in Table 4-4 and Table 4-5. The treatment of resistance within the framework of the particular organizational innovation model advocated in Chapter 2 seems to be much more explicit than the treatment of resistance within the scope of the major alternative models to be presented shortly. However, one very desirable activity was omitted; it involves connecting specific sources of resistance with the five major organizational variables discussed in Chapter 3. These variables are complexity, formalization, centralization, emphasis on interpersonal relationship, and conflict-resolution mechanisms. Ideally, we would have liked to discuss the relationship between need for stability, a possible source of resistance at the knowledge-awareness stage, with, say, formalization. One might postulate a relationship to the effect that the lower the degree of formalization, the greater the need for

Table 4-4.   Resistance and Stages of Organization Innovation Decision Making

Decision-Making Stage	Nature of Resistance
Knowledge awareness	Need for stability Coding scheme barrier Impact on existing social relationships Personal threat Local pride Felt need
Attitude formation and decision	Division of labor Hierarchical and status differences Physical separation of relevant parties
Initial implementation	Forces altering the innovation Feigned acceptance and utilization Conflict Passivity Perceived manipulation Felt mistrust of subordinates by superiors
Continued occurrence sustained imple- mentation	Continued conflict Occurrence of unintended dysfunctional effects Disillusionment because of false expectations

stability and hence the greater the likelihood this need will function as a source of resistance. Our review of the literature resulted in few generalizations that could be extended to any significant number of different contexts. It appears that the relationship between the sources of resistance and organization structure variables is situation bound. Existing data do not provide a foundation for going beyond specific cases although other scholars and future research may provide the necessary additional insight to develop generalizations. It is important, however, in a given situation for a manager to

Table 4-5.   Resistance of Stages
of Individual Innovation
Decision Making

Decision-Making Stage	Nature of Resistance
Perception	Selective processes
Motivation	Primacy
	Habit
Attitude	Illusion of importance
Legitimation	Dependence
Trial	Self-distrust
Evaluation	Insecurity
	Regression
	Anxiety
Adoption-rejection resolution	Homeostasis

consider how in his case resistance forces and structural characteristics interact.

REVIEW OF EXISTING THEORIES
OF INNOVATION IN ORGANIZATIONS

We now present a brief summary of selected theories of innovation, indicating how they fit with the theory presented in this book.

March and Simon

In beginning their discussion on innovation March and Simon (1958) emphasize the cognitive orientation of their theory by indicating their task as one of ". . . analyzing more completely how the cognitive limits on rationality affect the processes of organizational change and program development" (p. 172). The March and Simon theory tends to focus on problem solving and thus, as becomes clear below, describes the initiation phase of the innovation process but not the implementation phase.

In distinguishing between the continuation of an existing program of activity and innovation in that activity, they indicate that the former occurs primarily because the individual, group, or organization does not search for or consider alternative courses of action (p. 174). They emphasize that the persistence of existing activity is not caused by any particular type of resistance to change. Rather, it is the result of the absence of search for new alternatives because there is no dissatisfaction with existing programs (p. 174).

Innovations, then, occur when a given program of activity no longer satisfies performance criteria (p. 182). Organizational performance is now perceived as unsatisfactory. In Down's terms there is a performance gap—there is a discrepancy between what the organization is doing and what its decision makers believe it ought to or could be doing (Downs, 1966, p. 191). This dissatisfaction or performance gap, then, increases the search for alternative courses of action in March and Simon's model. In Chapter 2 of this book we discuss in detail the various ways in which discrepancies between what organization decision makers perceive the organization is doing and what they believe the organization could or ought to be doing in its performance. These causes of performance gaps are briefly summarized in Table 4–6.

Thus when this dissatisfaction with existing activity occurs as a result of performance gaps, search for alternative courses of action are started. The predicted result is that the organization is likely to become aware of new alternative courses of action, that is, innovations. From the preceding discussion, it appears that the March and Simon theory focuses on the initiation phase of the innovation process,

Table 4-6. Summary of Causes of
Performance Gaps

1. Adjustment of criteria of satisfaction to organization's level of performance is slow (March and Simon, 1958, p. 183)
2. Even in a stable environment the criteria of satisfactory performance are like aspiration levels in that they tend to adjust themselves upward (March and Simon, 1958, p. 183)
3. There may be changes in organization's *internal* environment: (1) new personnel may enter the organization; (2) technological changes may occur; (3) there may be shifts in power relationships
4. There may be changes in the organization's *external* environment: (1) the demand for the organization's output may have changed; (2) technological changes in the larger environment may occur (Downs, 1966, p. 172); (3) there may be changes in the organization's power position relative to other organizations

not on the process of implementation. Also, March and Simon do not attribute the persistence of any particular behavior to any general resistance to change. However, as stressed in Chapter 2, resistance to change is a major reason why many innovations never become implemented. As noted, the more radical the internal changes are that result from the implementation of an innovation the stronger the resistance will be. Thus for solution-radical innovations (reorientations) resistance to change cannot be ignored if the objective is to arrive at an understanding of the total process of innovation.

Burns and Stalker

Burns and Stalker's (1961) model provides a more macro focus on innovation because they examine how the organization deals with stable and changing environments. In their study of Scottish electronics organizations, they found that there was no one "best" type of organization structure for managing.

As spelled out in more detail in Chapter 3, Burns and Stalker indicate that when the environment is stable and fairly certain, the mechanistic type of organization is most appropriate for the organization (see Table 4-7). When the technical and market environment is changing and unstable, an organic type of organization (Table 4-7) is more appropriate because of its increased potential for gathering and processing information for decision making. Thus they show that there is no one best type of organizing for decision making. Rather, the mode of organizing is contingent on the decision situation.

Burns and Stalker also identify the role of resistance to change in explaining why an organization does not change its method of organization from mechanistic to organic when situations warrant it. They indicate that the political and status structures in the organization might be threatened as the organization changes and becomes more organic to deal with innovations. From Table 4–7, it can be seen that as an organization becomes more organic, there is more of a diffusion of authority, more participation in decision making, and so on, which could be a source of conflict and resistance if the organization were originally more mechanistic. However, they are relatively unclear in denoting the specific cause of these conflicts or resistance. For example, does the conflict arise from a mechanistic structure fighting a trend toward an organic system? Or does the conflict arise because diffusion of authority is a stage along the way toward an organic structure, a stage of development with which managers have not learned to cope?

Their theory seems to center on how organizations implement innovations. In emphasizing how the organic type of organization is better able to deal with innovative situations they focus on the various changes in the organization because of innovation. Again their theory, like that of March and Simon, is somewhat limited in that it does not note both the initiation and implementation stages of the innovation pro-

Table 4-7. Mechanistic and Organic Organizational Forms

Mechanistic	Organic
1. Tasks are broken into very specialized abstract units	1. Tasks are broken down into subunits, but relation to total task of organization is much more clear
2. Tasks remain rigidly defined	2. There is adjustment and continued redefinition of tasks through interaction of organizational members
3. Specific definition of responsibility that is attached to individual's functional role only	3. Broader acceptance of responsibility and commitment to organization that goes beyond individual's functional role
4. Strict hierarchy of control and authority	4. Less hierarchy of control and authority sanctions derive more from presumed community of interest
5. Formal leader assumed to be omniscient in knowledge concerning all matters	5. Formal leader not assumed to be omniscient in knowledge concerning all matters
6. Communication is mainly vertical between superiors and subordinates	6. Communication is lateral, between people of different ranks and resembles consultation rather than command
7. Content of communication is instructions and decisions issued by superiors	7. Content of communication is information and advice
8. Loyalty and obedience to organization and superiors is highly valued	8. Commitment to tasks and progress and expansion of the firm is highly valued
9. Importance and prestige attached to identification with organization itself	9. Importance and prestige attached to affiliations and expertise in larger environment

(Condensed from Burns and Stalker, 1961, pp. 119–122)

cess. The organization is viewed in a somewhat reactive sense in that we see how different types of organizations seem to be more effective in implementing innovations, but we are less clear as to how the organization became aware of the innovation and then decided to implement it using the type of structure it did.

Harvey and Mills

Harvey and Mills' (1970) theory focuses on patterns of organizational adaptation. Once again this theory tends to focus on the organizational processes involved in dealing with innovation. Harvey and Mills view the organization as a political system and indicate that change will result in some conflict between different units in the organization when a unit perceives that the change or innovation might reduce its influence (p. 184). Political coalitions are formed in the organization among subunits, and subunits remain committed to a change and innovation as long as there is something in it for them. Various types of bargaining take place between units as they try to improve their positions. Thus they begin to discuss conflict as it arises during innovation and identify bargaining processes as ways of reducing the conflict. However, they do not name the specific causes of either conflict or resistance.

Harvey and Mills also describe the kinds of problem situations the organization faces and the kinds of solutions the organization might implement. Both problem situations and problem solutions are arranged along a routine-innovative dimension. A routine solution is one the organization has used before "while an innovative solution is defined as a solution that has not been used before and for which there are no precedents in the organization" (pp. 189–190). Table 4–8 indicates the various combinations between problem situations and problem solutions.

The factors affecting the use of routine and innovative solutions are presented in Table 4–9 which is identical to Table 1.3. Harvey and Mills' rationale for the tendency to impose routine solutions on both types of problem situations is that the less pressure on the organization's "structural arrangements which emphasize predictability and stasis are likely to reinforce continuation of routine patterns around which interests have come to form rather than to promote innovative activity" (p. 191). On the other hand, when the contextual and internal variables appear as they do in the third column in Table 4–9 (a duplication of Table 1–3), the organization is in a higher stress-threat situation which is more likely to demand or require more innovative behavior if the organization is to adapt.

Harvey and Mills also do not mention the various phases of the innovation process in terms of initiation and implementation. However, they do discuss the sequences involved in the innovative problem–innovative solution process (pp. 194–199). There is *issue perception*, which identifies the event the organization needs to respond to. Once the event is defined there is a *formation of goals* of how the organization should respond. *Search* then occurs to determine which of the possible actions the organization might take is most appropriate. A *choice of a solution* is made on what course of action should be taken. Finally, there is *redefinition*, which may result in a choice of solution being modified because of pressures from other groups in the organization or as a result of information indicating that the current solution is not appropriate.

Table 4–10 indicates that Harvey and Mills' model focuses mainly on the initiation stage of innovation as specified in our model. There is little emphasis on the process of implementation except in their discussion of redefining the solution that is initially implemented.

Harvey and Mills elaborate on the models of March and Simon (1958) and Burns and Stalker (1960). Theirs is an

Table 4-8.　Problem Situations and
Solutions Encountered
by Organizations

Problem situation	Problem Solution	
	Routine	Innovative
Routine	A	B
Innovative	C	D

(Harvey and Mills, 1970, p. 190)

elaboration of March and Simons' model in that they emphasize the problem-solving process as it affects the selection of
the right type of solution for dealing with the problem situation the organization is experiencing. Harvey and Mills also
have a more organizational focus in their problem-solving approach as they view the political constraints that can operate
on the innovation process. Their model also elaborates on
Burns and Stalker's because they indicate that there are different types of problem solutions, mechanistic routine and organic innovative (i.e., ways of operating) that are appropriate
for different situations. They also go beyond Burns and
Stalker in specifying some of the contextual and internal variables that affect which type of solution is chosen to deal with
the type of situation the organization is facing (see Table 4-9).
Although they do not identify the structural characteristics of the routine and innovation solutions, their theory still
emphasizes that the organization's response is contingent on
the type of situation the organization is experiencing.

　　The shortcoming of the Harvey and Mills' model is that
they do not examine the characteristics of the organization,
other than its technology and communication structure, as
they affect the innovation process. There is no specification
of how the organization is structured, of the hierarchy of au-

Table 4-9. Internal and Contextual Variables Affecting the Use of Routine and Innovative Solutions on Both Routine and Innovative Problems

I Organizational Variables Affecting Propensity to Impose Particular Solutions on Particular Problems	II Tendency to Impose Routine Solutions on Both Types of Problems when:	III Tendency to Impose Innovative Solutions on Both Types of Problems when:
Contextual		
Size of organization relative to competitors	Relatively large	Relatively small
Age of organization relative to competitors	Relatively old	Relatively young
Degree of competition in market situation	Relatively uncompetitive market	Relatively competitive
Rate of technological change	Relatively slow	Relatively rapid
Internal		
Diffuseness of organization's technology (size of product line)	Relatively specific	Relatively diffuse
Degree of formalization of internal communication system	Relatively formalized	Relatively diffuse

(From Harvey and Mills, 1970, pp. 190–192.)

Table 4-10. Stages of the Innovation Process Compared

Harvey and Mills	Zaltman, Duncan, Holbek
Issue perception	I. Initiation stage
Formation of goals	1. Knowledge-awareness substage
Search	2. Formation of attitudes toward innovation substage
	3. Decision substage
Choice of solution	II. Implementation stage
Redefinition	1. Initial implementation
	2. Continued-sustained implementation

thority, centralization, complexity, and so on with respect to implementing routine and innovative solutions. Thus the process of actually dealing with innovation is unclear both theoretically and practically. Theoretically we do not know the dynamics of the innovation process. The practitioner is also left to discover the implications for translating this model into action. He is told there are different types of solutions for different types of situations, but he is not provided with insights into how he should structure the organization for innovative or routine solutions.

Wilson

Wilson emphasizes that the central aspect of the organization is its economy of incentives. "An incentive is any gratification, tangible or intangible, in exchange for which persons become members of the organization . . . and once in the organization, contribute time, effort, or other valued resources . . ." (Wilson, 1966, p. 196). The cost of an innovation is determined by the way incentives must be increased or redistributed (p. 197). With emphasis on the incentive system, the potential for conflict is clear because any innovation or change in the organization may result in members perceiving that their incentives will be affected.

Wilson discusses three stages of innovation, the *conception* of the change, the *proposing* of the change, and the *adoption and implementation* of the change. He predicts that the amount of innovation in these three stages is a function of the complexity of the existing task structure and incentive system (p. 198). The task structure becomes more complex as the "number of different tasks increases and as the proportion of nonroutine tasks increases" (p. 198). The incentive system increases in complexity as the number of sources of incentives increases (p. 199). He then offers several hypotheses on the diversity and complexity of the organization and innovation.

Wilson specifies that the greater the diversity and complexity of the organization in terms of task and incentives, the greater the likelihood that participants will both *conceive* of and *propose* innovations (p. 200). He points out that a highly diverse organization inhibits close supervision because it is difficult for the superior to completely monitor all the activities for his subordinates. Thus individuals have some flexibility in defining how they will do their job, and there are then more opportunities for them to become aware of ways to innovate.

One of Wilson's most important contributions is that he identifies the dilemma the organization faces in the innovation process. The diversity and complexity that increase the conceiving and proposing of innovations reduce the proportion of proposals that will be adopted. Wilson's explanation is that the high complexity makes it difficult for any one source of authority to achieve or force consensus toward agreement on which of the many proposals should be implemented (pp. 202–203). At the implementation stage there is, then, the potential for conflict and bargaining between different interest groups in the organization. He elaborates on the notion

that it is easier to initiate innovations than implement them in
stating that it is "easier to increase the organizations capacity
to generate new proposals than it is to increase its capacity to
ratify any given proposal" (p. 207). His theory again focuses
on the organization as the level of analysis. He also looks at
the complexity of the task and incentive systems as they affect the innovation process. However, he does not look at
other organizational structure characteristics such as formalization, and centralization.

One possible shortcoming of Wilson's model is his lack
of specification for ways of dealing with the innovation
dilemma—the fact that these factors that increase the potential for initiation reduce the potential for adoption or implementation. He does not provide much guidance for how
the practitioner might deal with this dilemma in terms of facilitating the implementation phase. Are there not some actions that the manager might take to facilitate both the initiation stage and the implementation process? It thus appears
that although Wilson specifies initiation and implementation
steps in his model, he mainly emphasizes the initiation stage in
providing guidelines for action. One is alerted to the fact that
conflict might occur during the implementation phases, but it
is less clear how one might respond to these problems.

Hage and Aiken

Hage and Aiken's (1970) work takes a definite organizational
focus and is closest to the theory developed in the present
book. Hage and Aiken go beyond the theories previously reviewed in that they focus on *both* the various stages of the innovation process as well as specifying several characteristics
of organizations as they affect program change in organizations. Program change is defined as ". . . the addition of new

services or products" (p. 13). This book has defined innovation as any idea, practice, or material artifact perceived to be new by the relevant unit of adoption. Thus the definition presented here goes beyond Hage and Aiken in that it specifies the point of reference for the new product or service. The product, service, and so on must be perceived as "new" by the adopting unit. Hage and Aiken identify seven organizational characteristics that affect the rate of innovation in organizations. We now present brief summaries of each of these as they relate to the rate of innovation.

Complexity. Complexity is defined by "the number of occupational specialties in the organization and the degree of professionalism of each" (Hage and Aiken, 1970, p 33). Hage and Aiken then predict that greater complexity leads to greater program change. The rationale for this is that (1) more professional employees are more likely to be concerned about keeping abreast of knowledge, which makes them more likely to recognize a need for change; (2) because of the existence of very different groups, the organization is likely to have more varied sources of information available for developing new programs (p. 37).

Centralization. Hage and Aiken (p. 38) define centralization as the concentration of power and decision making in the hands of a small proportion of individuals. They then predict that the higher the centralization, the lower the rate of program change. The supporting rationale for this is (1) when power is located in the hands of a few individuals, these individuals are less likely to experiment because they feel that they might lose their power; (2) more participation in decision making (less centralization) has the potential for bringing many diverse ideas forward that may identify new areas for change, but less participation does not; and (3) more decentralization also leads to conflict in perspectives for dealing with issues, which is likely to identify new areas for change (pp. 38–39).

Formalization. Hage and Aiken (p. 43) define formalization as the degree of codification of jobs in the organization. They then predict that the greater the formalization, the lower the rate of program change. The logic here is (1) that highly formalized rules offer little latitude to consider alternative ways about performing them; (2) that high emphasis on rules may discourage better alternative ways at performing because deviation may bring punishment; and (3) members may simply assume that existing rules offer the best way of performing (pp. 43–44).

Stratification. Stratification is defined by Hage and Aiken as the differential distribution of rewards to the jobs in the organization (p. 45). They predict that the greater the stratification, the lower the rate of program change. The rationale is that (1) change has the potential for diminishing differences among groups in the system so that the well-off are likely to resist and (2) high stratification decreases upward communication, especially of negative results because of fear of evaluation (pp. 45–46). There thus may be fewer opportunities to communicate upward the existence of performance gaps that might require innovation.

Production. Hage and Aiken define production as an indication of a high emphasis on quantity versus quality (p. 49). They predict that the higher the volume of production, the lower the rate of program change because (1) a high emphasis on quantity leads to a decision to avoid interruptions that often accompany innovations and (2) the trial and error that follow implementation reduce output—thus innovation will be avoided where strong emphasis on production exists. (pp. 49–50).

Efficiency. Efficiency refers to "relative emphasis on the cost reduction of the product or service" (p. 50). They believe that the greater the emphasis on efficiency, the lower the rate of program change. The rationale is that the implementation of innovations often involves unpredictable costs. The result is that there will be pressure to maintain the status quo.

Job Satisfaction. Satisfaction is defined as "the degree of morale among the job occupants in the organization" (p. 52). They forecast that the higher the job satisfaction, the greater the rate of program change because satisfied employees are more committed to the organization and therefore are more receptive to new ideas that might improve the organization (pp. 53–54).

In their theory Hage and Aiken also specify several stages of the innovation process. These are listed in Table 4–11 where they are compared with stages in our model. *Evaluation* is the first stage and consists of organizational decision makers (1) determining that the system is not accomplishing its goals as effectively as it could be and (2) chang-

Table 4-11. Comparison of Stages of the Innovation Process

Hage and Aiken	Zaltman, Duncan, Holbek
	Initiation stage
Evaluation	Knowledge-awareness substage
	Formation of attitudes toward innovation substage
	Decision substage
Initiation	
	Implementation stage
Implementation	Initial implementation substage
Routinization	Continued-sustained implementation substage

ing the goals of the system (Hage and Aiken, 1970, p. 94). Hage and Aiken do acknowledge that the evaluation stage is concerned with identifying performance gaps. However *initiation*, as specified by Hage and Aiken, tends to be more concerned with decision making and problem solving to find required job skills and financial support that are required for the innovation (pp. 97–99). *Implementation* is the initial attempt to integrate the innovation into the organization. Resistance and disequilibrium are likely to be high because of unexpected problems and sources of resistance that are likely to be encountered as the innovation is actually introduced. Here conflict is predicted to be high as lower level participants resist. *Routinization* follows the initial trial that took place in the implementation stage. In routinization the decision is made to retain the innovation and fully integrate it into the ongoing activities of the organization.

Thus Hage and Aiken emphasize both the characteristics of organizations that affect the rate of innovation as well as the stages of that process that go beyond the less-inclusive theories of March and Simon, Burns and Stalker, Harvey and Mills, and Wilson. However, there are still some gaps in their theory.

One of the shortcomings of their theory is that they do not identify the organizational dilemmas presented by the innovation process as identified initially by Wilson (1969) and elaborated upon by the model presented in Chapter 3 of this book. Hage and Aiken present their hypotheses concerning the relationships between the different organizational characteristics and rate of innovation but do not indicate that these relationships might vary, depending on the stage of the innovation process. For example, Hage and Aiken (1970, p. 33) predict that high complexity leads to greater program change. However, as indicated early in Chapter 3, this is contingent on the stage of the innovation process. During initiation the relationship is likely to hold because complexity increases the number of ideas and amount of information available to the organization, which is likely to increase the awareness and need for innovation. However, as Wilson (1966) has indicated, complexity can cause problems during implementation. In a complex organization individuals have very different backgrounds and expectations about what the organization should be doing. The result is that it may be very difficult for the organization to agree on what and how proposals should be implemented. This dilemma is not acknowledged by Hage and Aiken. They do not, as is pointed out in Chapter 3, indicate how the stages of the innovation process might affect the relationships between organization characteristics and rate of innovation. Their theory thus is somewhat static and less powerful in offering suggestions to the practitioner as to managing the innovation process.

SUMMARY AND CONCLUSIONS

The theory presented in this book has focused on the innovation process at the level of the organization. The initiation and implementation stages of the innovation process are identified and discussed in Chapter 2, followed by the characteristics of the organization as they affect the innovation process in Chapter 3. In comparison to the theories of March and Simon, Burns and Stalker, Harvey and Mills, Wilson, and Hage and Aiken, the theory presented here has attempted to focus on the dynamics and to provide guidelines for facilitating both the initiation *and* implementation stages of the innovation process. We acknowledge the innovation dilemma specified by Wilson (1966, p. 200), but we do not think it is unresolvable. We list the specific characteristics of the organization that have the potential for facilitating the initiation and implementation stages, the felt need for organizational innovation change, and the communicating of this innovation to the relevant parties. The decision substage incorporates the innovation search and selection processes. The adoption of the most appropriate solution or innovation combines both the initial and the sustained implementation stages.

One final comment should be added. Chapter 1 contains a brief discussion of an overall model of organizational changes and innovation and a paradigmatic representation of it in Figure 1-1. This figure is repeated here as Figure 4-1. It is worth noting what aspects of this overall model are covered by the different theories of organizational change presented in this chapter. March and Simon give considerable attention to the performance gap and the search for solutions, and they also highlight the possibilities that the initial impetus for innovation can be either external or internal to the organization. Their theory is somewhat "vague," however, about the function of persuading other members of the organization that innovation is needed and about the processes of adoption and rejection. Burns and Stalker are strongest in discussing the decision-making and adoption and rejection processes but are relatively weak in explicit considerations concerning performance gaps, felt needs, and the identification of alternative solutions. As noted earlier in this chapter, Harvey and Mills give relatively little attention to the adoption and/or rejection stages but emphasize stages of felt need (issue perception), solution search, and selection (identification of most appropriate alternatives). Wilson seems to be more comprehensive in covering the various factors in Figure 4-1 than March and Simon, Harvey and Mills, or Burns and Stalker. However, not unexpectedly, the model advocated in Chapter 2 is much closer to the sequence of activities in Figure 4-1. Change in ·the external environment and the perception of this change produce the knowledge-awareness substage. The performance gap is also established at this stage, regardless of the time sequence of problem-awareness first versus innovation-awareness first. The attitude-formation stage involves the

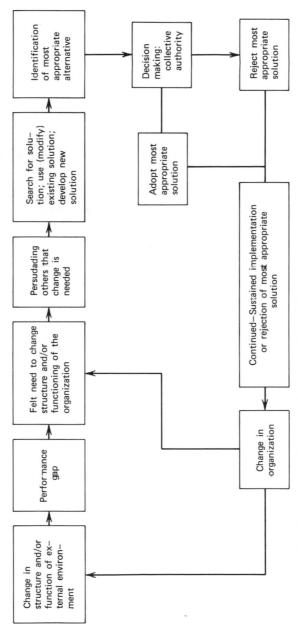

Figure 4-1. Paradigm of organizational change and innovation.

felt need for organizational innovation and the communicating of this innovation to other relevant parties. The decision substage incorporates the innovation search and selection processes. The adoption of the most appropriate solution or innovation combines both the initial and the sustained implementation stages.

NOTES

1. It should be noted here that there are various other potential mediators such as the nature of the task, resources available to the organization, and influence of the organization over its environment. Future research should identify these more specifically.

Bibliography

Achilladelis, B., P. Jervis, and A. Robertson (1971). *Report on Project SAPPHO to the Science Research Council: A Study of Success and Failure in Innovation.* Sussex, England: Science Policy Research Unit, University of Sussex.

Aguilar, Francis J. (1967). *Scanning the Business Environment.* New York: Macmillan.

Allvine, Fred C. (1968). "Diffusion of a Competitive Innovation," in R. King, Ed., *Proceedings of the American Marketing Association,* pp. 341–351.

Argyris, Chris (1970). *Intervention Theory and Method.* Reading, Mass.: Addison-Wesley.

Argyris, Chris (1965). *Organization and Innovation.* Homewood, Ill.: Dorsey Press.

Argyris, Chris (1964a). *Integrating the Individual and the Organization.* New York: Wiley.

Argyris, Chris (1964b). "T-Groups for Organizational Effectiveness," *Harvard Business Review,* 42, No. 2: 60–75.

Argyris, Chris (1962). *Interpersonal Competence and Organizational Effectiveness.* Homewood, Ill.: Irwin-Dorsey.

Baker, Norman R., Jack Siegman, and Albert H. Rubenstein (1967). "The Effects of Perceived Needs and Means on the Generation of Ideas for Industrial Research and Development Projects," *IEEE Transactions on Engineering Management,* EM-14: 156–163.

Bandura, Albert (1969). *Principles of Behavior Modification.* New York: Holt, Rinehart and Winston.

Barnett, H. G. (1953). *Innovation: The Basis of Culture Change.* New York: McGraw-Hill.

Bavelas, Alex (1950). "Communication Patterns in Task Oriented Groups," *Journal of the Acoustical Society of America,* 22: 725–730.

Bean, Alden (1972). "Coupling the Management Science Function to User Groups: Some Observations on the Implementation of Management Science Projects in the Marketing Area." Ph.D. dissertation, Graduate School of Management, Northwestern University.

Becker, M. H. (1970). "Sociometric Location and Innovativeness: Reformulation and Extension of the Diffusion Model," *American Sociological Review, 35* (April): 267–282.

Becker, Selwyn, and Thomas L. Whisler (1967). "The Innovative Organization: A Selective View of Current Theory and Research," *The Journal of Business, 40*, No. 4: 462–469.

Beckhard, Richard (1969). *Organization Development: Strategies and Models.* Reading, Mass.: Addison-Wesley.

Bell, W. (1963). "Consumer Innovators: A Unique Market for Newness," *Proceedings of the American Marketing Association:* 85–95.

Bennet, C. (1969). "Diffusion Within Dynamic Populations," *Human Organizations, 28* (Fall): 243–247.

Bennis, Warren (1966). *Changing Organizations.* New York: McGraw-Hill.

Bennis, Warren (1963). "A New Role for the Behavioral Sciences: Affecting Organizational Change," *Administrative Science Quarterly, 8:* 125–165.

Bertalanffy, Ludwig von (1968). *General System Theory.* New York: George Braziller.

Blake, Robert, and Jane Mouton (1969). *Building a Dynamic Corporation Through Grid Organizational Development.* Reading, Mass.: Addison-Wesley.

Blake, Robert, Herbert Shepard, and Jane Mouton (1964). *Managing Intergroup Conflict in Industry.* Houston: Gulf Publishing Co.

Blau, Peter, and W. Richard Scott (1962). *Formal Organizations: A Comparative Approach.* San Francisco: Chandler Publishing Co.

Blau, Peter (1960). "Orientation Toward Clients in a Public Welfare Agency," *Administrative Science Quarterly, 5:* 341–361.

Blau, Peter (1956). *The Dynamics of Bureaucracy.* New York: Random House.

Bradshaw, Barbara, and C. Bernell Mapp (1972). "Consumer Participation in a Family Planning Program." *American Journal of Public Health, 62*, No. 7 (July): 972–989.

Brandner, L., and B. Keal (1964). "Evaluation for Congruence as a Factor in the Adoption Rate of Innovations,"*Rural Sociology, 29:* 288–303.

Burns, Tom, and G. M. Stalker (1961). *The Management of Innovation.* London: Tavistock Publications.

Cadwallader, Mervyn (1959). "The Cybernetic Analysis of Change in Complex Organizations," *American Journal of Sociology, 65:* 154–157.

Campbell, D. T. (1969). "Reforms as Experiments," *American Psychologist* (April): 409–422.

Campbell, Rex R. (1966). "A Suggested Paradigm of the Individual Adoption Process," *Rural Sociology, 31* (December): 458–466.

Caplow, Theodore (1964). *Principles of Organization.* New York: Harcourt Brace Jovanovich.

Carlson, R. O. (1968). "Summary and Critique of Educational Diffusion Research," *Research Implications for Educational Diffusion,* Michigan Department of Education.

Carroll, Jean (1967). "A Note on Departmental Autonomy and Innovation in Medical Schools," *Journal of Business, 40,* No. 4: 531–534.

Carter, Charles, and Bruce Williams (1957). *Industry and Technical Progress: Factors Governing the Speed of Application of Science.* London: Oxford University Press.

Cartwright, Dorwin (1965). "Influence, Leadership, Control," in J. G. March, Ed., *Handbook of Organizations.* Chicago: Rand McNally, pp. 1–47.

Chandler, Alfred (1962). *Strategy and Structure.* Cambridge, Mass.: MIT Press.

Coch, L., and J. R. P. French, Jr. (1948). "Overcoming Resistance to Change," *Human Relations, 1:* 512–532.

Coe, Rodney M., and Elizabeth A. Barnhill (1967). "Social Dimensions of Failure in Innovation," *Human Organization, 26,* No. 3 (Fall): 149–156.

Collins, Barry, and Harold Guetzkow (1964). *A Social Psychology of Group Processes for Decision Making.* New York: Wiley.

Conrath, David W. (1968). "The Role of the Informal Organization in Decision Making on Research and Development," *IEEE Transactions on Engineering Management, EM-15,* No. 3: 109–119.

Cooke, Robert A. (1972). Personal communication.

Corwin, Ronald (1969). "Patterns of Organizational Conflict," *Administrative Science Quarterly, 14:* 507–522.

Crain, R. (1966). "Fluoridation: The Diffusion of an Innovation Among Cities," *Social Forces, 44* (June): 467–476.

Coughlan, Robert, and Gerald Zaltman (1972). "Implementing the Change Agent Team Concept." Paper presented at American Educational Research Association Conference.

Coughlan, Robert J., Robert A. Cooke, and L. Arthur Safer, Jr. (1972). *An Assessment of a Survey Feedback—Problem Solving—Collective Decision Intervention in Schools*. Final Report, U.S. Office of Education, Small Grants Division, Area V. Project NO. O-E-105 Contract NO. OEG-5-70-0036 (509).

Cyert, R. M., and J. G. March (1963). *A Behavioral Theory of the Firm*, Englewood Cliffs, N.J.: Prentice-Hall.

Czepiel, John A. (1972). "The Diffusion of Major Technological Innovation in a Complex Industrial Community: An Analysis of Social Processes in the American Steel Industry." Ph.D. dissertation, Northwestern University.

Dalton, G. W. (1968). *The Distribution of Authority in Formal Organization*. Boston: Harvard University Division of Research.

Derr, C. Brooklyn (1972). "Conflict Resolution in Organizations: Views from the Field of Educational Administration," *Public Administrative Review*, XXXII: 495–502.

Deutsch, K. W. (1963). *The Nerves of Government: Models of Political Communication and Control*. New York: The Free Press.

Dill, William (1958). "Environment as an Influence on Managerial Autonomy," *Administrative Science Quarterly*, 2: 409–443.

Downs, Anthony (1966). *Inside Bureaucracy*. Boston: Little, Brown and Company.

Duncan, Robert B. (1973). "Multiple Decision Making Structures in Adapting to Environmental Uncertainty: The Impact on Organizational Effectiveness," *Human Relations* (Volume 26, in press).

Duncan, Robert B. (1972a). "Characteristics of Organizational Environments and Perceived Environmental Uncertainty," *Administrative Science Quarterly*, 17: 313–327.

Duncan, Robert B. (1972b). "Organizational Climate and Climate for Change in Three Police Departments: Some Preliminary Findings," *Urban Affairs Quarterly*, 8, No. 2, 205–246.

Dymsza, William (1972). *Multinational Business Strategy*. New York: McGraw-Hill.

Eicholtz, Gerhard, and Everett M. Rogers (1964). "Resistance to the Adoption of Audiovisual Aids by Elementary School Teachers," in Mathew Miles, Ed., *Innovation in Education*. New York: Teachers College Press, Columbia University.

Elbing, A. D. (1970). *Behavioral Decisions in Organizations*. Glenview, Ill.: Scott, Foresman.

Emery, R. E., and E. Trist (1965). "The Causal Texture of Organizational Environments," *Human Relations, 18:* 21–31.

Evans, R. I. (1970). *Resistance to Innovation in Higher Education*. San Francisco: Jossey-Bass Publishers.

Federal Trade Commission (1967). "Permissible Period of Time During Which New Products May be Described as 'New,'" *Advisory Opinion Digest No. 120* (April 15).

Festinger, Leon (1957). *A Theory of Cognitive Dissonance*. Evanston, Ill.: Row, Peterson.

Fliegel, F. C., J. E. Kivlin, and G. S. Sekhon (1968). "A Cross-Cultural Comparison of Farmers' Perceptions of Innovations as Related to Adoption Behavior," *Rural Sociology, 33* (December): 437–449.

Foster, George (1962). *Traditional Cultures and the Impact of Technological Change*. New York: Harper & Row.

French, Wendell, and Cecil Bell, Jr. (1973). *Organization Development: Behavioral Science Interventions for Organization Improvement*. Englewood Cliffs: Prentice-Hall.

Gameson, William H. (1966). "Rancorous Conflict in Community Politics," *American Sociological Review*.

Georgopoulos, Basil S. (1972). "The Hospital as an Organization and Problem-Solving System" in B. S. Georgopoulos, Ed., *Organization Research on Health Institutions*. Ann Arbor, Mich.: Institute for Social Research.

Gibb, Jack R. (1961). "Defensive Communication," *The Journal of Communication, 11* (September): 141–148.

Ginzburg, E., and E. Reilly (1957). *Effective Change in Large Organizations*. New York: Columbia University Press.

Golembiewski, Robert, and Arthur Blumberg, Ed. (1970). *Sensitivity Training and the Laboratory Approach*. Itasca, Ill.: F. E. Peacock Publishers.

Goodenough, Ward Hunt (1963). *Cooperation in Change*. New York: Russell Sage Foundation.

Graham, Saxon, "Cultural Compatibility in the Adopting of Television," *Social Forces 33*, No. 2 (December 1954).

Graziano, Anthony M. (1969). "Clinical Innovation and the Mental Health Power Structure: A Social Case History," *American Psychologist, 24*, No. 1 (January): 10–18.

Griffiths, Daniel (1964). "Administrative Theory and Change in Organizations," in Matthew Miles, Ed., *Innovation in Education.* New York: Bureau of Publication, Teachers College, Columbia University.

Gross, Neal, Joseph B. Giacquinta and Marilyn Bernstein (1971). *Implementing Organizational Innovations: A Sociological Analysis of Planned Educational Change.* New York: Basic Books.

Grossman, Joel B. (1970). "The Supreme Court and Social Change," *American Behavioral Scientist 13*, No. 4.

Guetzkow, Harold, and W. R. Dill (1957). "Factors in the Development of Task Oriented Groups," *Sociometrey, 10:* 175–204.

Guetzkow, Harold, and Herbert Simon (1955). "The Impact of Certain Communication Nets Upon Organization and Performance in Task Oriented Groups," *Management Science:* 233–250.

Hage, Jerald, and Michael Aiken (1970). *Social Change in Complex Organizations.* New York: Random House.

Hage, Jerald, and Michael Aiken (1967). "Program Change and Organizational Properties: A Comparative Analysis," *American Journal of Sociology, 72*, No. 5: 503–519.

Hagen, E. E. (1962). *On the Theory of Social Change.* Homewood, Ill.: Dorsey Press.

Hall, Richard H. (1962). "The Concept of Bureaucracy: An Empirical Assessment," *American Journal of Sociology, 69:* 32–40.

Harvey, Edward, and Russell Mills (1970). "Patterns of Organizational Adaptation: A Political Perspective," in Mayer N. Zald, Ed., *Power in Organizations.* Nashville, Tenn.: Vanderbilt University Press.

Havelock, Ronald G. (1970). *Planning for Innovation.* Ann Arbor: Center for Research on Utilization of Scientific Knowledge, University of Michigan.

Herman, Charles (1963). "Some Consequences of Crisis Which Limit the Viability of Organizations," *Administrative Science Quarterly, 8:* 61–82.

Hoffman, L. Richard, and N. R. F. Maier (1961). "Quality and Acceptance of Problem Solutions by Members of Homogeneous and Heterogeneous Groups," *Journal of Abnormal and Social Psychology, 62:* 401–407.

Homans, G. C. (1961). *Social Behavior: Its Elementary Forms.* New York: Harcourt Brace and Jovanovich.

Hornstein, Harvey, Barbara Bunker, Warner Burke, Marion Gindes, and Ray Lowicki, Eds. (1971). *Social Intervention: A Behavioral Science Approach.* New York: The Free Press.

Hutchins, L. (1972). *Management Training Units.* San Francisco: The Far West Laboratory for Educational Research and Development.

Jacoby, Jacob (1971a). "Multiple-Indicant Approach for Studying New Product Adopters," *Journal of Applied Psychology, 55* (August): 384–388.

Jacoby, Jacob (1971b). "Personality and Innovation Proneness," *Journal of Marketing Research, 8* (May): 244–247.

Jones, Garth N. (1969). *Planned Organizational Change.* New York: Frederick A. Praeger.

Juris, Hervey, and Peter Feuille (1973). *Police Unions: Power and Impact in Public Sector Bargaining.* Lexington, Mass.: D. C. Heath–Lexington Books.

Kahn, Robert, Donald Wolfe, J. D. Snoek, and Richard Rosenthal (1964). *Organizational Stress: Studies in Role Conflict and Ambiguity.* New York: Wiley.

Kahneman, D., and E. O. Schild (1966). "Training Agents of Social Change in Israel: Definition of Objectives and a Training Approach," *Human Organization, XXV:* 71–77.

Katz, Daniel, and Robert Kahn (1966). *The Social Psychology of Organizations.* New York: Wiley.

Kelley, Harold, and John Thibaut (1969). "Group Problem Solving," in Gardner Lindzey and Elliot Aronson, Eds., *The Handbook of Social Psychology Second Edition*, Volume 4. Reading, Mass., Addison-Wesley, pp. 1–102.

Kelman, Herbert C., and Donald P. Warwick (1973). "Bridging Micro and Macro Approaches to Social Change: A Social-Psychological Perspective," in G. Zaltman, Ed., *Processes and Phenomena of Social Change.* New York: Wiley Interscience.

194   Bibliography

Klein, Donald (1967). "Some Notes on the Dynamics of Resistance to Change: The Defender Role," in G. Watson, Ed. Concepts for Social Change. Washington, D.C.: NTL Institute for Applied Behavioral Science.

Klonglan, Gerald, and Walter Coward, Jr. (1970). "The Concept of Symbolic Adoption: A Suggested Interpretation," *Rural Sociology, 35* (March): 77–83.

Knight, K. (1967). "A Descriptive Model of the Intra-Firm Innovation Process," *Journal of Business, 40* (October): 478–496.

Knight, K., and Yoram Wind (1968). "Innovation in Marketing: An Organizational Behavior Perspective," *California Management Review 11*, 1.

Köhler, J. W. L. (1969). "The Case History of the Research on the Stirling Cycle," in *The Process of Technological Innovation*. National Academy of Engineering, Washington, D.C.: National Academy of Sciences.

Lavidge, R. J., and G. A. Steiner (1961). "A Model for Predictive Measurements of Advertising Effectiveness," *Journal of Marketing, 25*.

Lawrence, Paul R., and Jay Lorsch (1967a). "Differentiation and Integration in Complex Organizations," *Administrative Science Quarterly*.

Lawrence, Paul, and Jay Lorsch (1967b). "New Management Job: The Integrator," *Harvard Business Review, 45*, No. 6: 142–151.

Lin, Nan, and Gerald Zaltman (1973). "Dimensions of Innovations," in G. Zaltman, Ed., *Processes and Phenomena of Social Change*. New York: Wiley Interscience.

Linton, R. (1936). *The Study of Man*. New York: Appleton-Century-Crofts.

Lippitt, Jeanne Watson, and Bruce Westley (1958). *The Dynamics of Planned Change*. New York: Harcourt Brace and Jovanovich.

Lippitt, R. (1965). "Roles and Processes in Curriculum Development and Change," in *Strategy for Curriculum Change*. Washington, D.C.: Association for Supervision and Curriculum Development.

Littaner, D., A. F. Wessen, and J. Goldman (1970). "Evaluating Change in Systems of Child Feeding," in R. M. Coe, Ed., *Planned Change in the Hospital*. New York: Praeger.

Litwak, Eugene (1961). "Models of Bureaucracy Which Permit Conflict," *American Journal of Sociology, 67*: 177–184.

Lynton, Rolf P. (1969). "Linking an Innovative Subsystem into the System," *Administrative Science Quarterly, 14,* No. 3: 398–416.

Maier, N. R. F. (1970). *Problem Solving and Creativity: In Individuals and Groups.* Belmont, Calif.: Brooks/Cole Publishing Co.

Mann, Floyd C. (1957). "Studying and Creating Change: A Means to Understanding Social Organization," *Research in Industrial Human Relations,* Industrial Relations Research Association, No. 17: 146–167.

March, James, and Herbert Simon (1958). *Organizations.* New York: Wiley.

Marquis, Donald G., and Sumner Myers (1969). *Successful Industrial Innovations.* Washington, D.C.: National Science Foundation, U.S. Government Printing Office.

Marrow, Alfred, David Bowers, and Stanley Seashore (1967). *Management by Participation.* New York: Harper and Row.

Menzel, II. (1960). "Innovation, Integration, and Marginality: A Survey of Physicians," *American Sociological Review, 25.*

Merton, Robert K. (1940). "Bureaucratic Structure and Personality," *Social Forces, 23:* 560–568.

Miller, James G. (1965). "Living Systems: Basic Concepts," *Behavioral Science, 10:* 193–237.

Miller, Roger E. (1971). *Innovation, Organization and Environment.* Sherbrooke: Institut De Recherche et De Perfectionnement en Administration, Université de Sherbrooke.

Milo, Nancy (1971). "Health Care Organizations and Innovation," *Journal of Health and Social Behavior, 12:* 163–173.

Mohr, Lawrence (1969). "Determinants of Innovation in Organizations," *American Political Science Review, 63:* 111–126.

Mueller, W. F. (1962). "The Origins of the Basic Inventions Underlying Du Pont's Major Product and Process Innovations, 1920–1950," in R. R. Nelson, Ed., *The Rate and Direction of Inventive Activity: Economic and Social Factors.* Princeton: Princeton University Press, pp. 323–360.

Myers, S., and D. G. Marquis (1969). *Successful Industrial Innovations.* National Science Foundation: NSF 69-17.

McWhinney, William (1968). "Organizational Form, Decision Modalities and the Environment," *Human Relations, 21:* 269–281.

National Academy of Sciences (1969). *The Process of Technological Innovation,* Washington, D.C.

Neal, Rodney, and Michael Radnor (1971). "The Relationship Between Formal Procedures for Pursing OR/MS Activities and OR/MS Group Success." Paper delivered at 40th National Conference of the Operations Research Society of America at Anaheim, California (October), pp. 25–29.

Normann, R. (1971). "Organizational Innovativeness: Product Variation and Reorientation," *Administrative Science Quarterly, 16*, 2.

Olson, M. (1971). "Preliminary Thoughts About the Causes of Harmony and Conflict." Unpublished paper, University of Maryland.

Pareek, Udal, and Y. P. Singh (1969). "Communication Nets in the Sequential Adoption Process," *Indian Journal of Psychology, 44:* 33–55.

Paul, B. (1961). "Fluoridation and the Social Scientists: A Review," *The Journal of Social Issues, XVII*, No. 4.

Parsons, Talcott (1956). "Suggestions for a Sociological Approach to the Theory of Organizations-1," *Administrative Science Quarterly, 1:* 63–85.

Pellegrin, Roland J. (1969). "The Place of Research in Planned Change," in Richard O. Carlson, et al., Eds., *Change Processes in the Public Schools.* Eugene, Oregon: Center for the Advanced Study of Educational Administration, pp. 65–75.

Pellegrin, Roland J. (1966). *An Analysis of Sources and Processes of Innovation in Education.* Eugene, Oregon: Center for the Advanced Study of Educational Administration, p. 32.

Pelz, Donald G., and Frank M. Andrews (1966). *Scientists in Organizations: Productive Climates for Research and Development.* New York: Wiley.

Perrow, Charles (1972). *Complex Organizations: A Critical Essay.* Glenview, Ill.: Scott, Foresman.

Pohlman, Edward (1971). *Incentives and Compensations in Birth Planning.* University of North Carolina: Carolina Population Center.

Pugh, D. S., D. J. Hickson, C. R. Hinings, and C. Turner (1968). "Dimensions of Organization Structure," *Administrative Science Quarterly, 13*, No. 1: 65–106.

Radnor, Michael, and Rodney Neal (1971). "The Progress of Management Science Activities in Large U.S. Industrial Corporation." Program publication #4-71 Cooperative International Program of Studies of Operations Research and the Management Sciences, Evanston, Ill., Northwestern University.

Radnor, Michael, Albert Rubenstein, and David Tansik (1970). "Implementation in Operations Research and R&D in Government and Business Organization," *Operations Research*, *18*, No. 6: 967–991.

Radnor, Michael, Albert Rubenstein, and Alden Bean (1968). "Integration and Utilization of Management Science Activities in Organizations," *Operations Research Quarterly*, *19*: 117–141.

Read, William (1962). "Upward Communication in Industrial Hierarchies," *Human Relations*, *15*: 3–15.

Rice, A. (1963). *The Organization and Its Environment*. London: Tavistock Publication.

Robertson, Thomas (1971). *Innovative Behavior and Communication*. New York: Holt, Rinehart and Winston.

Rogers, Everett M. (1973). "Social Structure and Social Change," in G. Zaltman, Ed., *Processes and Phenomena of Social Change*. New York: Wiley Interscience.

Rogers, Everett M. (1972a). *Field Experiments on Family Planning Incentives*. Ann Arbor: University of Michigan, Dept. of Communications (May).

Rogers, Everett M. (1972b). "The Ernakulam Vasectomy Campaigns," Michigan State University, mimeo.

Rogers, Everett M., and F. Floyd Shoemaker (1971). *Communication of Innovations: A Cross-Cultural Approach*. New York: The Free Press.

Rogers, Everett M. (1969). *Modernization Among Peasants: The Impact of Communication*. New York: Holt, Rinehart and Winston.

Rogers, Everett M. (1962). *Diffusion of Innovations*. New York: The Free Press.

Rokeach, Milton (1968). *Beliefs, Attitudes, and Values*. San Francisco: Jossey Bass.

Roos, Noralou P., and Victor Berlin (1972). "A Causal Model of Organizational Decision Making." Working paper 119-72, Northwestern University.

Rothe, H. (1960). "Does Higher Pay Bring Higher Productivity?" *Personnel*, *37*: 20–38.

Sanders, J. T. (1961). "The Stages of a Community Controversy: The Case of Fluoridation," *Journal of Social Issues, XVII*, No. 4.

Sapolsky, Harvey (1967). "Organizational Structure and Innovation," *Journal of Business, 40*, No. 4: 497–510.

Schein, Edgar (1970). *Organizational Psychology: Second Edition.* Englewood Cliffs, N.J.: Prentice-Hall.

Schein, Edgar (1969). *Process Consultation: Its Role in Organization Development.* Reading, Mass.: Addison-Wesley.

Schon, Donald (1967). *Technology and Change.* New York: Dell.

Schroder, Harold, Michael Driver, and Siegfried Streufert (1967). *Human Information Processing.* New York: Holt Rinehart and Winston.

Seashore, Stanley, and Ephraim Yuchtman (1967). "Factorial Analysis of Organizational Performance," *Administrative Science Quarterly, 12:* 377–396.

Selznick, Philip (1949). *TVA and the Grass Roots.* Berkeley: University of California Press.

Shepard, Herbert A. (1967). "Innovation-Resisting and Innovation Producing Organizations," *Journal of Business, 40*, No. 4: 470–477.

Shull, Fremont, Andre Delbecq, and L. Cummings (1970). *Organizational Decision Making.* New York: McGraw-Hill.

Sills, D. (1957). *The Volunteers: Means and Ends in a National Organization.* New York: The Free Press.

Simon, Herbert A. (1957). *Models of Man.* New York: Wiley.

Spicer, Edward H. (1952). *Human Problems in Technological Change* (ed.). New York: Russell Sage Foundation.

Stephenson, Robert W., Benjamin S. Gantz, and Clara E. Erickson (1971). "Development of Organizational Climate Inventories for Use in R&D Organizations," *IEEE Transactions on Engineering Management*, EM-18, No. 2.

Steiner, Gary (1965). *The Creative Organization.* Chicago: University of Chicago, Graduate School of Business.

Stewart, Michael (1957). "Resistance to Technological Change in Industry," *Human Organization, 16*, No. 3 (Fall): 36–39.

Stiles, Lindley J., and Beecham Robinson (1973). "Change in Education," in G. Zaltman (ed.), *Processes and Phenomena of Social Change.* New York: Wiley Interscience.

Straus, M. A. (1970). "Family Organization and Problem Solving Ability in Relation to Societal Modernization," *Köhner Zeitschrift für Soziologie*, Supplement 14.

Straus, Robert (1972). "Hospital Organization from the Viewpoint of Patient-Centered Goals," in Basil S. Georgopoulos, Ed., *Organization Research on Health Institutions*. Ann Arbor: University of Michigan, Institute for Social Research.

Stufflebeam, Daniel (1967). "The Use and Abuse of Evaluation in Title III," *Theory into Practice 6:* 126–133.

Summers, Gene F. (1970). "Introduction," in Gene F. Summers (ed.), *Attitude Measurement*. Chicago: Rand McNally.

Sykes, A. J. (1962). "The Effects of Supervising Training Course in Changing Supervisors Perceptions and Expectations of the Role of Management," *Human Relations, 15:* 227–243.

Taylor, Donald W. (1965). "Decision Making and Problem Solving," in James March, Ed., *Handbook of Organizations*. Chicago: Rand McNally.

Taylor, J. (1970). "Introducing Social Innovation," *Journal of Applied Behavioral Science, 6:* 69–77.

Terreberry, Shirley (1968). "The Evolution of Organizational Environments," *Administrative Science Quarterly, 12:* 590–613.

Thio, A. O. (1971). "A Reconsideration of the Concept of Adopter Innovation Compatibility in Diffusion Research," *The Sociological Quarterly, 12* (Winter): 56–68.

Thompson, James D. (1967). *Organizations in Action*. New York: McGraw-Hill.

Thompson, James, and Arthur Tuden (1959). "Strategies, Structures and Processes of Organizational Decision," in J. Thompson, E. Hammond, R. Hawkes, B. Junker, and H. Tuden, Eds., *Comparative Studies in Administration*. Pittsburgh: University of Pittsburgh Press, pp. 195–217.

Thompson, Victor A. (1969). *Bureaucracy and Innovation*. University, Alabama: University of Alabama Press.

Thompson, Victor (1961). *Modern Organization*. New York: Alfred A. Knopf.

Tilton, John E. (1971). *International Diffusion of Technology: The Case of Semiconductors*. Washington, D.C.: The Brookings Institute.

Torrance E. Paul (1961). "A Theory of Leadership and Interpersonal Behavior Under Stress," in Luigi Petrullo and Bernard Bass, Eds., *Leadership and Interpersonal Behavior*. New York: Holt, Rinehart and Winston, pp. 100–118.

Utterback, James M. (1971a). "The Process of Technological Innovation Within the Firm," *Academy of Management Journal, 14,* No. 1: 75–88.

Utterback, James (1971b). "The Process of Innovation: A Review of Some Recent Findings," in George Wilson, Ed., *Technological Development and Economic Growth*. Bloomington, Ind.: School of Business, Division of Research, pp. 139–160.

Walker, J. L. (1969). "The Diffusion of Innovations Among the American States," *American Political Science Review, 63.*

Walton, Richard, John Dutton, and Thomas Cafferty (1969). "Organizational Context and Interdepartmental Conflict," *Administrative Science Quarterly, 14:* 522–544.

Warwick, Donald P., and Herbert C. Kelman (1973). "Ethical Issues in Social Intervention," in G. Zaltman, Ed., *Processes and Phenomena of Social Change*. New York: Wiley Interscience.

Watson, Goodwin (1973). "Resistance to Change," in G. Zaltman, Ed., *Processes and Phenomena of Social Change*. New York: Wiley Interscience.

Watson, Goodwin (1971). "Resistance to Change," *American Behavioral Scientist, 14:* 745–766.

Weber, Max (1947). *The Theory of Social and Economic Organization*. Translated by A. M. Henderson and T. Parsons. New York: The Free Press.

Weick, Karl (1969). *The Social Psychology of Organizing*. Reading, Mass.: Addison-Wesley.

Whyte, William F. (1969). *Organizational Behavior: Theory and Application*. Homewood, Ill.: Irwin-Dorsey.

Wilson, James Q. (1966). "Innovation in Organization: Notes Toward a Theory," in James D. Thompson (ed.), *Approaches to Organizational Design*. Pittsburgh: University of Pittsburgh Press, pp. 193–218.

Yancy, William L. (1970). "Intervention as a Strategy of Social Inquiry: An Exploratory Study with Unemployed Man," in L. A. Zurcher and C. M. Bonjean, Eds., *Planned Social Interventions*. New York: Chandler Publishing Co.

Yeracaris, C. A. (1961). "Social Factors Associated with the Acceptance of Medical Innovations: A Pilot Study," *Journal of Health and Social Behavior*, 3: 193–198.

Young, Cliff (1972). "Marketing Interfaces in Organization." Unpublished doctoral dissertation, Northwestern University.

Yuchtman, Ephraim, and Stanley Seashore (1967). "A System Resource Approach to Organizational Effectiveness," *American Sociological Review*, 32, No. 6: 891–903.

Zaltman, Gerald, and Robert Duncan (forthcoming). *Strategies for Planned Changes*. New York: Wiley.

Zaltman, Gerald, and George Brooker (1971). *A New Look at the Adoption Process*, working paper Northwestern University.

Zaltman, Gerald, Philip Kotler, and Ira Kaufman, *Creating Social Change*. New York: Holt, Rinehart, and Winston.

Zaltman, Gerald, and Ronald Stiff (1973). "Theories of Diffusion," in S. Ward and T. Robertson, Eds., *Theoretical Perspectives in Consumer Behavior*. Englewood Cliffs, N.J.: Prentice-Hall.

Zaltman, Gerald, and Barbard Köhler (1972). "The Dissemination of Task and Socioemotional Information in an International Community of Scientists," *Journal of the American Society for Information Science*, 34, No. 4 (July–August): 225–236.

Zaltman, Gerald, and Bernard Dubois (1971). "Problems and Conceptual Innovations." Paper presented at the Second Annual Meeting of the Association for Consumer Research (September 1–3).

AUTHOR INDEX

SUBJECT INDEX

Halo effect, 93
Harvey and Mills' model of alternative, situations and solutions, 25
Harvey and Mills' theory of innovation, 172-176
Hierarchical differentials, 89
Hierarchy of authority, 121-123; *also see* Centralization

Idea generation stage, 118
Immanent change, 6
Implementation stage, 66-70
  cross-unit comparison, 69-70
  change-agent intervention, 67-68
  definition, 58-59
  feedback mechanism, creation of, 77-78
  innovation decisions, class of, 78-85
  organization structure and activity during, 133-154
  problems, anticipation of, 75-77
  radicalness, problems related to, 78
  resistance during, 90-94
  substages of, 66-70
  theories of innovation, in other, 167-186
  Zaltman, Duncan, Holbek theory, in, 158-167
Incentive, 16
  based in decision group, 81
  definition, 16
  innovation behavior, 90, 112
  organization, central aspect of, 176-178
  stratification as rewards, 180
  types of, 16
Individual-oriented models, 61
  Colley's model, 61
  Klonglan and Coward's model, 61
  Lavidge and Steiner's model, 61
  Robertson's model, 61
  Rogers' model, 61
  Rogers and Shoemaker's model, 61
  Zaltman and Brooker's model, 61
Individual resistance, 94-103
Information processing, classes of innovation, decisions, related to, 81
  decisions substage, in, 66
  feedback, 71-78
  interpretation, need for, 77-78
  organizational environment, affected by, 114-121
  organizational structure, affected by, 121-154
  resistance to, 85-103
  theories of innovation, in other, 167-186

Zaltman, Duncan, Holbek theory, in, 158-167
Initial cost, 33
Initial implementation stage, 67, 78, 164-166
  resistance during, 90-92
  trial of potential adoption, 67
Initiation stage, 60-66
  classes of innovation decision related to, 78-85
  cross-unit comparison, 69
  definition, 58
  diffusion theory, 58
  iterative process, 71
  organizational structure and activity during, 133-154
  problems, 75-77
  resistance during, 86-87
  substages of, 60-66
  theories of innovation, in other, 167-186
  Zaltman, Duncan, Holbek theory, in, 158-167
Innovation, attributes of, 32-45
  definitions, 7-16, 165
  orientation of, 14-16
Innovation classification, 78-79
Innovation dissonance, 64-66
  definition, 64
  dissonant adopter, 64-65
  dissonant rejector, 64-65
  resolution of, 100-103
Innovation process, 58-70
  circularity, 70-71
  control of, by feedback, 70-78
  individual-oriented models, 61
  innovative decisions, 78-85
  organization-oriented models, 62
  organizational environments, affected by, 110-121
  organizational structure, affected by, 121-154
  resistance to, 85-103
  stages of, 58-70
  theories of innovation, in other, 167-186
  Zaltman, Duncan, Holbek theory, in, 158-167
Innovative solution, *see* Radical solution; Reorientation
Innovation(radical) situation, 23
Innovation, theories of, 158-185
  Burns and Stalker, 169-172
  Hage and Aiken, 178-183
  Harvey and Mills, 172, 176
  March and Simon, 167-169
  Wilson, 176-178
  Zaltman, Duncan, Holbek, 158-167

Performance gaps, 55-58
  definition, 2-3, 55
  due to change in, criteria of satisfaction, 55-56
    internal environment, 56
    external environment, 57-58
  organization characteristics, affected by, 134-143
  performance achievement, 55
  theories of innovation, in other, 167-186
Performance radical innovation, 30-31
Personal threat, 86
Pervasiveness, 37, 48
Physical separation, 89-90
Point of origin, 40-41, 163-165
Policy innovation, 15
Political processes in decision making, 78-85
Potential for innovation, perception of, 64
Power, shifts in, 56-58
Precocity, 10
Preference ordering, 53
Primacy, 97
Process evaluation (feedback), 74
Product evaluation (feedback), 74
Product innovation, 14
Production, 180
Production-process innovation, 14
Programmed innovation, 17-21, 31
Promotion and selection based on technical competence, 123
Publicness versus privateness, 44, 164-165
  collective adoption/rejection, 49

Radicalness, 19, 23-32
  definition, 19-20
  organizational environments, affected by, 110-121
  organizational structure, affected by, 121-154
  radical solution, 24-28, 30-31, 47, 72-73, 78
  theories of innovation, in other, 167-186
  Zaltman, Duncan, Holbek theory, in, 158-167
Rational behavior, need for, 147-148;
    also see Interpersonal relationships
Redefinition, 173
Rejection, 99-100
Reliability, 39
Reorientation, 27, 30-31, 48, 72
  impact on sybsystems, 29-30
  types of, 30
  also see Radical solution

Resistance, 85-104, 165-167
  decisions, and classes of, 78-85
  individual, 94-103
  instrumental innovation, 23
  organizational environments, affected by, 110-121
  organizational structure, affected by, 121-154
  substages, during, 85-94
  theories of innovation, in other, 167-186
  Zaltman, Duncan, Holbek, in, 165-167
Resolution, 100-103
Returns to investment, 35-36, 164-165
Reversibility, 42
Reward, see Incentive
Risk and uncertainty, 36, 163-165
Risk, 54
  risk taking, 147
Robertsons' model of innovation process, 61
Rogers' model of innovation process, 61
Rogers and Shoemaker's model of innovation process, 61
Rogers' paradigm of types of social change, 6
Role conflict, ambiguity, 89, 139-142
Routine solution, 23
  impact on subsystems, 29-30
  variation, 27
  also see Radicalness
Routinization, 181-182
Rules and procedures, system of, in bureaucracy, 122-155; also see Formalization

Schein's adaptive-coping cycle, 70-71
Scientific status, 39, 163-165
  subattributes of, 39
Scope, 24, 27, 47
Search, 3, 5, 173
  general model of organizational, 20
Seashore and Yuchtman's performance factors, related to ability to exploit resources, 108-109
Selective contact change, 6
Sequencing, rate of, 79
  sequencing of phases, 67, 69, 81
Services innovation, 14
Shepard's model of innovation process, 62
Situation radicalness, 23-24; also see Radicalness
Slack innovation, 17-18, 31
Social change, definition of, 2, 14
  paradigm of types of, 6
  related to innovation, 4-6
  also see Change